A Look at Life
FROM A
Deer Stand

DEVOTIONAL

Steve Chapman
Author of *A Look at Life from a Deer Stand*

HARVEST HOUSE PUBLISHERS

EUGENE, OREGON

Cover photo © Charles J. Alsheimer

Cover by Koechel Peterson & Associates, Inc., Minneapolis, Minnesota

A LOOK AT LIFE FROM A DEER STAND DEVOTIONAL
Some devotions adapted from Steve Chapman,
With God on a Deer Hunt.
Copyright © 2009 by Steve Chapman
Published by Harvest House Publishers
Eugene, Oregon 97402
www.harvesthousepublishers.com

ISBN 978-0-7369-2548-8 (padded hardcover)
ISBN 978-0-7369-5474-7 (Milano Softone™)

Printed in China

12 13 14 15 16 17 / RDS-SK / 16 15 14 13 12 11

This book is dedicated to you.
It is my prayer that you
will be strengthened and encouraged
in your walk with God.

Acknowledgments

A very heartfelt thanks be to God who has given us the gift of His creation so we can learn about Him, our Maker.

A special thanks to Annie for sending me "Out there!" The cookies are always good.

A word of appreciation to those who let me enjoy their property.

Thank you to Pastor Bill Rudd at Calvary Church in Fruitport, Michigan, for the insights that inspired "Twice Amazed" and "He Can, Can He?"

A note of thanks to John MacArthur for his commentary on the book of James that yielded the thoughts in "Look Intently."

Contents

1. Jackson's Wait 7

2. Life in the Leaf 11

3. The Slap 14

4. The Farmer and the Field 17

5. Don't Give In 20

6. The Grunt Call 23

7. The Markings 27

8. Look Intently 30

9. The Oxygen Mask ..34

10. In the Spotlight 38

11. When God Goes Hunting 41

12. The Drive-Through ..44

13. The Watch 48

14. A Select Arrow 51

15. A Sound like a Frog 54

16. Skin and Ink 57

17. The Snort 60

18. Song of the Hunter ..63

19. The Look 66

20. What to Wear? 70

21. Prime Time 74

22. Skipping in the Dark 77

23. Little Foxes and Big Toenails 81

24. Safety Belt 85

25. Attacked! 89

26. Whiter Than Snow 93

27. Popsicles 97

28. The Trail 100

29. Apple Seeds 104

30. Words 108

31. And So They Prayed 112

32. Fall Blend 116

33. Pick a Spot 119

34. He Never Did Anything 123

35. Twice Amazed ...127

36. Straight to the Pantry 130

37. He Can, Can He? ..134

38. Thanks, Adam! 137

39. Bottle and Book ...141

40. The Condo 144

41. Middle Seat 148

42. Guilty 'Til Proven
    Innocent 152

43. Scoot Over 156

44. Seize the Moment . . 160

45. Leaves of Three,
    Let It Be 164

46. Next Time 168

47. Not Just Walking . . 173

48. The Shell 177

49. Still Yielding 181

50. That Boy of Mine . . 185

51. The Bones Testify . . 189

52. The Comparison . . 192

53. The Strike 195

54. The Watcher 199

55. When the Wolf
    Comes Near 204

56. Waking the
    Dawn 207

57. When I Hear that
    Train 210

58. The Ant War 214

59. Gone Green 219

60. Answers Require
    Questions 223

61. East and West 226

62. Finish Well 230

63. The Invitation 234

64. The Web 238

65. Benny and Joe 243

66. Dancers and
    Singers 246

67. Follow the Blood . . 250

68. Grease Is Cheaper . . 253

69. I Wanna Go with
    My Daddy 256

70. Jack 260

71. Just Two Words . . . 264

72. We Saw the
    Evidence 267

73. Hunting on
    Credit 272

74. A Country Boy
    Testifies 277

75. What's on Your
    Mind? 281

    Lyric Credits 285

1

Jackson's Wait

This is the day which the LORD has made;
let us rejoice and be glad in it.

PSALM 118:24

Jackson is an inquisitive, five-year-old neighbor boy who showed up one summer day in my backyard as I was preparing to practice with my compound bow. "What ya doin'?" was the first of a thousand questions.

As I removed my bow and arrows from the case, his eyes widened. I instructed him to stand safely behind me as I took a few shots. Stride for stride he followed me back and forth as I shot and retrieved my arrows. The conversation was endless. And this would not be the last time I would have company as I practiced that summer. I suspected that the seeds sown during our time together might someday yield a full-grown hunter.

Finally deer season arrived and, as I had promised Jackson, I managed to deliver a load of venison to his family. As I stood in their kitchen describing the hunt, Jackson was listening. The look on his face revealed a youthful hunger to go into the woods that demanded a response.

"Jackson, would you and your dad like to sit in a ground blind with me next week?"

He nearly passed out with excitement as he looked at his parents with that "Oh! Please don't say no!" look. They didn't refuse him, so we set a date and I went home. Little did I know what a dilemma I had created for their entire family. For days Jackson woke up and went to bed asking, "How much longer till I go hunting?" His dad described the torture to me later, and we had some chuckles over it. (At least I did.)

Having raised two children, I suppose I should have known better than to ask him so early. However, time had erased the memory of what kids are like when they are intensely anticipating an event. Time creeps too slowly. Hours are weeks, and days are months. Jackson's inability to wait patiently wore heavily on the nerves of everyone around him. I even got a taste of it whenever he showed up under our second floor patio: "We still goin' huntin', Mr. Chapman?" He was relentless. He could be comforted only by one answer: "Sure are, little buddy!"

As grueling as the wait might have been for my

young neighbor (and his family), there was something beautiful about it. Romans 8:19 states that creation itself "waits eagerly for the revealing of the sons of God." Because of the distortion that sin brought into humanity's relationship with God, the earth "groans" (not a complaining sound, but a sigh at the reality of living in a sinful world) for redemption. It longs to know the uncorrupted presence of those whose spirits belong to a holy God.

The day will come when all of creation—including our aching, aging bodies—will be set free from the slavery of deterioration. Until it comes to pass, there is only one hope that can comfort our anxious hearts. It is knowing that our spirits have already been redeemed as a result of another day that was eagerly anticipated—"when the kindness of God our Savior and His love for mankind appeared, He saved us" (Titus 3:4-5). That was the greatest day the Lord ever made!

Oh, my blessed Redeemer, blessed be the day You appeared with salvation for the sons and daughters of man. As I sit in the midst of creation and contemplate its longing for redemption, I rejoice

that I am already Your own. With an anticipation that rivals that of an excited child, I am waiting for You to come and restore this earth to Your glory. In Jesus, my Deliverer's name, I pray. Amen.

2

Life in the Leaf

*He will be like a tree firmly planted
by streams of water, which yields its fruit
in its season and its leaf does not wither.*

PSALM 1:3

When deer hunting season returns, summer is behind us and the foreboding winter lies ahead. It is autumn, a time when something sober begins to happen to the leaves that have been alive since the spring. A certain dry curl at their edges silently speaks of their impending demise. Though still mostly green at the end of September, the life source is slowly being drawn from them. There is no way to stop the process.

I am well over 50 years old now. It feels like my "autumn" has arrived. There's a peculiar dryness about my joints that is troublesome. Other body parts are showing the effects of the years, especially my hairline. Bones that didn't ache before are speaking to me. As far as my eyes are concerned, forget the longer arms idea—pass me my glasses! I feel like my friend who has a birthday close to mine. We're the same age. When I asked him how it felt, he responded, "Hey! I feel like a teenager..." He paused for a moment then added with a tired sigh, "...that's been in a wreck!"

Thankfully, though the body is undeniably decaying, Psalm 1 offers every human the hope of being like a tree with eternal foliage. But there are prerequisites. They are found in the first two verses of the chapter: "How blessed is the man who does not walk in the counsel of the wicked, nor stand in the path of sinners, nor sit in the seat of scoffers! But his delight is in the law of the LORD, and in His law he meditates day and night."

I want to be that man—bold enough to avoid the pitfall of listening to the lies of those who do not embrace the wisdom of the Lord. I want to walk close to my Creator and not stand where sinners tread back and forth to their wickedness. For that reason, today I will take advantage of the quietness of the deer stand to ponder the mandates and the ways of my God. As I search the woods with my eyes, I will scan the Scriptures stored in my heart and meditate on God's truth. In them, my "leaves" will find life.

Lord, thank You for the privilege of coming into Your presence. As I bring Your truth to my remembrance, teach me in these quiet moments so that my life's roots can burrow even deeper into the security of knowing You. In Jesus, my Lifegiver's name, I pray. Amen.

3

The Slap

Arise, O LORD; save me, O my God!
For You have smitten all my enemies on the cheek;
You have shattered the teeth of the wicked.

PSALM 3:7

Not too many hunts ago, I was sitting quietly in my treestand growing angrier by the minute at the mosquitoes that were driving me insane. One of the pesky bugs landed on my face and started boring into my upper jaw. Disregarding the risk of too much motion or noise, I slapped the stupid thing and mashed it before it deposited too much venom. Unfortunately, I also managed to seriously rattle my own cage. As I was recovering from the self-inflicted blow to my poor head, I thought of the story my wife, Annie, tells about the day she silenced an enemy.

The younger, obnoxious brother of an older, nasty-minded fellow mercilessly teased her during a morning bus ride to high school. It was not the first time he'd tortured her with comments that falsely accused her of being attracted to his deviant elder brother. It was humiliating and embarrassing, and it continued as the bus rolled down the highway. However, the siege against Annie's crumbling emotions soon came to an abrupt end. She had had enough.

Annie faced her accuser in his seat and stared squarely into his eyes. Then, without any consideration for her safety or reputation, she drew back her right arm as far as she could and released the string on an unbelievably forceful slap across the face of her nemesis.

On impact, she claims, the boy's eyes that were crossed became uncrossed for a brief moment. The sound of the hand-on-cheek explosion was deafening. The sudden noise of teeth banging violently against one another was excruciating to hear. The deed was done. Only the low roar of the heavy tires on pavement filled the bus until it arrived at school.

That happened more than 30 years ago and to this day, somewhere in the hills of West Virginia, the echo of that slap is still bouncing through time. The outcome? Never again was Annie teased by the young snit whose lights were so significantly dimmed, even if only momentarily. Though she readily admits her retaliation was not the most appropriate way to handle the situation, I'm proud of my wife for her courage. (And I try to never make her mad!)

Annie's slap on the jaw of the kid that provoked her is a vivid picture of today's verse. Some of us may have enemies who are spreading rumors about us or adversaries determined to undermine our businesses. Some may even have foes who want to do bodily harm. Isn't it great that we can say, "Blessed is the one who comes to the defense of our souls and shuts up our accusers!" And we can praise God for the outcome of His deliverance: "Salvation belongs to the LORD; Your blessing be upon Your people!" (Psalm 3:8).

Lord, thank You for hearing my spirit's cries for help. Your hand is mighty and able to deliver. Only You can silence my enemies. Please come to my defense; my deliverance belongs to You. You alone are the shield for my soul and the lifter of my head in the face of my accusers. In the blessed name of Christ I pray. Amen.

4

The Farmer and the Field

*The seed in the good soil, these are the ones who
have heard the word in an honest and good heart,
and hold it fast, and bear fruit with perseverance.*

LUKE 8:15

The trails were well used but the ground around them was unmarked by bedding depressions and droppings. The deer were passing through but not stopping on my little piece of property. I decided a food plot might entice them to linger for a while, and with good deerstand placement, my few acres could hold some promise for a successful hunt come October.

I picked out an area along a creek bed and cleared some timber so the sunlight would reach the ground. Before hauling a heavy, gas-powered tiller into the remote spot, I tested the soil with my three-pound mattock. When I lifted the heavy tool over my head and brought it down into the dirt I struck rock. My teeth rattled and my vision blurred upon impact.

Everywhere I dropped the mattock I heard the telltale steel-on-stone sound. I knew the job would be bigger than I had planned.

For the next several days it was dig and throw, dig and throw. I guess I tossed at least 1,000 softball-sized stones into the creek. And the various roots I had to dig up were long and tangled. It was an exhausting process. On the third day of preparing the ground, I thought of the chorus of a song I had written several years before when my children were much younger. It is titled "The Farmer and the Field" and it goes like this:

> He was the farmer, I was the field
> And it always hurt when the ground was tilled
> But he was getting rid of the rocks and the weeds
> So the ground would be good when he sowed the seed.

The lyrics are the words of a wise son spoken in honor of an earthly father who was diligent to discipline him when he had done wrong. The dad was careful to do so because he understood that only "good soil" is able to successfully receive the imperishable seed of the Word of God. He was aware that the ground of the human heart is made good only through the hauling away of the rocks and weeds that would choke the seed. The son's wise father also knew another important element of being a parent/farmer: Compassion must accompany correction. While my rocky food-plot-to-be may not feel the forceful blows of my weighty mattock, the human heart does not escape the pain. The son's compliments to his dad indicated that the father had done well.

What was the result? Like my now green-and-delicious quarter of an acre, the dad harvested a son whose life displayed the fruit of the eternal seed of the Scriptures. Taking the time to prepare the soil of a child's heart is worth the effort!

Lord, thank You for being my kind Father. And thank You for the children You have given me. Please help me be diligent to discipline. I pray for Your mercy and compassion to flow through me as I prepare their hearts for Your good seed. And on that day when I finally see the fruit of my labor, I'll give You the glory. In Jesus' name I pray. Amen.

5

Don't Give In

Do not give the devil an opportunity.

EPHESIANS 4:27

One of the places I'm privileged to hunt is about 60 miles from my house. Occasionally, as I start up the entrance ramp to the highway, I think of a story I once heard:

An old southern farmer who looked and sounded like "Mr. Haney" on the classic TV show *Green Acres,* was in his rattletrap truck approaching the entrance to a busy, city freeway. As he puttered onto the four-lane, a well-dressed businessman barreling down the road in his fancy, late-model sports car suddenly slammed into him. The two men exited their wrecked vehicles. The raging city slicker stomped over to the farmer.

"Hey, you crazy hick! Didn't you see the yield sign?"

The farmer removed his dirty hat, scratched his head as he surveyed the damage to his truck, and replied with an indignant country drawl, "I *yield* at ya three times, mister, and ya wouldn't git over!"

Now there's a man who had set his course and was not about to be deterred. Though his simple-minded oversight of the laws of the highway cannot be defended, the seasoned country gentleman has to be admired for his unwavering determination.

When it comes to the enticements that the enemy of my soul offers, I want to be like that old farmer. I want to ignore the yield signs. The opportunity to make a decision like this came one day several years ago when a man challenged my attitude about maintaining social exclusivity with my wife. He thought my stance about never being alone with another woman in a public or private setting was archaic and prudish. His suggestion was to "branch out, be a free spirit." Without hesitation I dismissed his advice as misleading and dangerous. His counsel reminded me of Colossians 2:8: "See to it that no one takes you captive through philosophy and empty deception, according to the tradition of men, according to the elementary principles of the world, rather than according to Christ." Another passage warns, "If sinners entice you, do not consent" (Proverbs 1:10). And still another says, "The wisdom of this world is foolishness before God" (1 Corinthians 3:19). Not too many months after the man offered his poisonous opinion, I learned he had been caught in an adulterous affair and was eventually served with divorce papers. I felt sorry for him, but I did feel justified in not yielding my position.

Perhaps the next time you venture onto a freeway and see one of those triangle-shaped signs that say "Yield," you'll remember the old farmer and think of the words of wisdom: "Do not give the devil an opportunity."

Father, I bring to You a heart of gratitude for the strength You provide to help me say a firm no to the enemy of my soul. Whatever the cost, may all the roads of relationships and pursuits that I enter find me unyielding to any bad advice and misdirection the world may offer. In Jesus' name I pray. Amen.

6

The Grunt Call

My sheep hear My voice,
and I know them, and they follow Me.

JOHN 10:27

It was a red-letter day for me when, for the first time, a buck responded to my grunt call. I'll never forget how he suddenly appeared about 45 yards in front of my treestand. He was walking in the openness of a logging road. Instead of leaving it and coming toward me on the trail that passed near my stand, he continued moving from my left to right at too far a distance for my arrow.

Because my nerves tend to turn into a bowl of shaky Jello when a deer appears, I almost forgot about the grunt call that was hanging on the lanyard around my neck. When I finally remembered it was there, it was nearly too late. As the deer stepped into the woods on the other side of the road and began to head away from my position, I quickly scrambled to get the call to my mouth.

When I pushed the air through the tube the

sound it made was meant to say, "Hey! I'm one of you! Over here. Stop. Come back!"

At the familiar sound of the call, the buck halted in his tracks and looked directly toward my stand. His uncanny ability to key in on my location was amazing. He stood for a few seconds, showed only a slight interest in what he had heard, then turned and once again started walking away.

I sent a second, gentler blast of air through the call.

Once more he stopped and looked my way. His pause was slightly longer, but he seemed determined to continue in the opposite direction. When he turned yet again to leave I blew once more. This time my heart nearly jumped out of my shirt when he wheeled around on his back hooves and started toward my stand. I carefully lowered the call to my chest, attached my release to the string, and prepared for the shot. I was already standing and by the time I came to full draw the buck was about 12 yards from my tree. The rest of the story is wrapped up and stored safely in my freezer.

I was absolutely amazed that I, a human, could connect vocally with such an animal as the elusive whitetail deer. Using a manmade device I had actually spoken to a creature that is not just different from me in degree, but in kind. He and I had nothing in common except that we both occupied space on the planet. The deer would not someday evolve into a man, nor would I, through many reincarnations, return someday as a whitetail. Yet I "spoke" to that deer and he answered. Incredible!

As I pondered the extraordinary fact that I had managed to communicate with the buck, I thought of how amazing it is that God can speak to people. We are also vastly different in kind. Yet God fully knows how to bridge the gap between Himself and humans. It is astounding to realize we can actually hear Him speak.

In John 10, a beautiful analogy is given regarding God's relationship to mankind. Those who follow Him are referred to as His sheep and God is called the Good Shepherd. In verse 4 it is a written that four-legged sheep follow their master because they know his voice. "A stranger they simply will not follow, but will flee from him, because they do not know the voice..." (verse 5). This physical picture of a spiritual reality shows the marvelous truth that mankind is able to "key in" on God's call to his heart.

When do we hear Him? Romans 8:16 points out, "The Spirit Himself bears witness with our spirit that we are children of God." You may be wondering if you have ever heard His voice. Was there ever a time when you were headed down the road of sin and had turned away from God in disobedience? Somewhere deep inside your heart did you hear, "Don't go that way. It is wrong! Turn around!" At that moment, did you stop and look to the Lord? If so, you heard the voice of the Good Shepherd. He who is eternal connected with you in that moment. And if you turned back toward Him, you were divinely enticed like a buck to a grunt call.

Unlike deer hunters who use our artificial calls to draw in a deer to *take* its life, Jesus calls us to Himself so that He can *give* us everlasting life. That, my friend, is the Good News! Have you responded to His call?

My God and the Keeper of my soul, thank You that You call out to the hearts of people. I pray to always hear You when You speak. I ask for discernment to know when it is not Your voice. Help me always come Your way when You call. In Jesus' name. Amen.

7

The Markings

I am fearfully and wonderfully made.

PSALM 139:14

Back in the 70s, my uncle, David Chapman, purchased a 30-30 caliber rifle. During a visit with him last year, he offered to sell it to me. Without hesitation I took him up on it. Why? Because the gun was not just a standard issue rifle. There was a special inscription on the barrel that read, "Winchester–Model 94/NRA Centennial Model/1871–1971." The gun had never been fired, and it was in mint condition. I thought about shooting a few rounds through it just to say I was the first to feel its smooth kick; however, I decided to keep it in its most valuable state. It is now safely stored and gaining daily in value as it ages toward antiquity in its protective case.

Perhaps someday in the distant future someone might even end up appearing with it on one of my wife's favorite TV programs, the *Antiques Roadshow*, which features appraisals of items of age and uniqueness. On occasion, viewers get to see some interesting looks on the faces of those who present their treasures. Annie loves it when they gasp in pleasant surprise that the thing they thought was worth only a few dollars turns out to be appraised for a figure that exceeds a five-year total of their annual income.

For example, one lady took a lamp to the show that had hideous lizards formed in stained glass on its shade. I fully agreed with Annie's reaction when she saw it: "I wouldn't put that thing in my house if you paid me. How ugly!" Then the appraiser turned the lamp over and there it was: *Tiffanys of New York!* Suddenly the lackluster lamp became an item worth fighting for. Annie's next response was, "Well…just maybe I could find a place for it somewhere in the house."

How a piece is marked makes all the difference. It's true for antiques and it's certainly true for humans. Other people might look at us and see only our unsightly features. Physical imperfections, limited abilities, a past that haunts us, lack of wealth, and other flaws that are unattractive might justify their negative appraisal of us. However, if they look under the surface and into our hearts they will find that distinguishing mark that makes onlookers sit up and take notice. They are the words written in Psalm 139:14: "fearfully and wonderfully made."

What we look like, what we have or don't have, and what others think of us do not determine our value. Instead, it's the mark of the God who made us that gives us distinct and ultimate worth. With that in mind, may we be careful to look at ourselves as well as those around us not according to the outward, fleshly appearance but in regard to the spirit of God that dwells inside.

Dear Lord, I thank You that I am fearfully and wonderfully made. Please help me remember this comforting truth when I am tempted to appraise my worth by the standards of the world. Help me recognize those around me the way You see them—priceless by design. In Jesus' name. Amen.

8

Look Intently

But one who looks intently at the perfect law,
the law of liberty, and abides by it, not having
become a forgetful hearer but an effectual doer,
this man will be blessed in what he does.

JAMES 1:25

Whitetail hunters who spend enough time in the woods where there is plenty of good cover for the animals sooner or later encounter a most intriguing phenomenon. Even though the foliage may be dense, there are times when a deer can slip within a few yards of a person and stand there totally undetected. Portions of their motionless form might show, but the hunter may never see it. Not knowing it is there, he could decide to scratch his nose—and the discernible gesture will likely send the wary critter scampering away!

I have had times when I was scanning the woods looking for movement when suddenly a spot in the brush that was light and open a few moments before is now dark and closed. I have visually gone on by it and continued my radarlike search. Then, as if the information is on a five-second delay, a bell in my brain goes off. My eyes return to the spot, and I peer at it for more than a little while. Then, lo and behold, there's an eye with that familiar, pale-white circle around it staring through the opening. As I study it closer and follow the lines, I see the tip of an ear. Upon closer examination of the immediate area below the ear and eye, I see sticks that amazingly turn into fur-covered legs.

At that point my heart rate soars, and I have to control my breathing and fight the urge to quickly raise my bow or gun. Oh! How I love it when that vague shape suddenly transforms into a deer. Knowing that I have been astute enough to take the necessary time to look closely and not miss the details is a most rewarding feeling. It's one of those things that keeps me going back to the woods year after year.

The way that a close inspection of heavy foliage often reveals a well-hidden deer and gets a hunter's pulse to rise is the same way a close look at the Scriptures can expose truth and inspire the reader. In today's passage, the words "looks intently" have a stronger meaning than you may realize. In the original language, it refers to stooping over and carefully peering at something from all possible vantage points. It's the way Peter looked into the empty tomb; he gave it a very thorough examination. Someone who looks into the Scriptures in this way will not only discover life-altering truths, but he will be so moved by them that a change of heart occurs. The individual becomes not just a reader, but a doer of the Word.

One who looks at the Word of God and goes on unchanged is described as a person who looks at himself in a mirror, turns away, and immediately forgets what kind of person he is. While he may have clearly seen his own image, he is either quickly distracted or uninterested. Tragically, the benefits of the Word of God in this person's life is lost. (See verses 23-24.)

It's impossible to know how many deer I have never seen because I didn't make the effort to really study the woods. And when it comes to the Scriptures, I shudder to think what I have missed as a result of reading it with no particular motivation other than curiosity or just "getting in a daily quota." I want to do better. I have a feeling you do too.

Thank You, Lord, for Your Word. It is filled with the truth about Your marvelous love and

amazing ability to save us. Help me not only see deeper into Your Word, but also to be a doer of what You reveal. May none of Your truths be lost to casual eyes. I ask for Your strength and patience to look intently at Your sayings. In Jesus' name. Amen.

9

The Oxygen Mask

Then I will teach transgressors Your ways,
and sinners will be converted to You.

PSALM 51:13

I suppose it seems strange that I enjoy climbing into the heights of a treestand to hunt but truly dislike flying in airplanes. The truth is, the actual ascent doesn't bother me, it's the steady flying that leaves me tired and tense. Though it saves time and wear and tear on my body, my emotions take a beating when I fly. I'm one of those people who returns a look of terror when someone asks, "What's your *final* destination?" (I wish they wouldn't use that word!) And when a person asks, "Do you have reservations?" my standard response is a nervous, "Should I? Is there something wrong with the plane? Of course I have reservations! I don't want to get on it!"

Because of my ongoing resistance to being a projectile wildly hurled through the skies at breakneck speeds, I am always attentive to the safety speech the flight attendants give before takeoff. While others read their newspapers or talk to their neighbors, my eyes are usually focused on the front of the cabin. On one particular flight, as the lady attendant was delivering her safety sermon, a certain word caught my ear. I had just read a Scripture that used it. The word was "then." She used it this way:

> In the unlikely event of a loss of cabin pressure, a panel will open above you and a mask will fall down. Reach up, take the mask, place it over your nose and mouth, adjust the tabs, and breathe normally. [Right!] If you have a child with you, put the mask on yourself first, *then* assist your child.

In Psalm 51, David's cry for God's cleansing after he sinned with Bathsheba is recorded. He begs, "Wash me thoroughly from my iniquity and cleanse me from my sin...Wash me, and I shall be whiter than snow...And blot out all my iniquities. Create in me a clean heart, O God, and renew a steadfast spirit within me. Do not cast me away from Your presence" (Psalm 51:2,7,9-11). Finally, verse 13 begins with the particular word that caught my ear: "*Then* I will teach transgressors Your ways." (Though *then* is not in the original language, it is appropriately included.)

That day on the airplane a life-changing thought occurred to me. When the flight attendant gave the instructions regarding the masks and children, her discourse was more profound than she might have realized. In it was a picture of the order we are to follow if we care about the spiritual well-being of our children. In a world that is in trouble and morally spiraling out of control, parents must be the first to take in the life-giving breath of Christ. There is no way we can effectively assist our kids if we are spiritually unconscious. We need to let God cleanse our hearts from our sins and cause us to have willing spirits to let Him do it daily. It is crucial that we lean on Him for purification so we can better teach our "little transgressors" His ways.

Dear Lord, thank You for allowing me this time in Your presence. Forgive me for my offenses to You. It is against You, and You alone, that I have sinned. Cleanse and renew me. As a parent, I seek the joy of Your forgiveness so that I, in turn, can lead my children to know it as well. You teach that it is the "prayers of a righteous man that accomplishes much." Help me, by Your

grace, to be a pursuer of holiness. Without it, I am unable and unqualified to lead my children to the life-giving breath You want to breathe into their lives. In Your name I pray. Amen.

10

In the Spotlight

Many are saying, "Who will show us any good?"
Lift up the light of Your countenance
upon us, O LORD.

PSALM 4:6

I suspect nearly all of us have inadvertently spotlighted deer with our headlights. Those green,
glowing eyes in the high beams are an immediate
giveaway of an animal's presence. It is always a delight
to behold such an illusive creature, even in the artificial ray of manmade sunshine.

I wonder how it feels to be spotlighted. Do the
deer ask, "What possible thrill can those humans get
out of blinding us this way?" I suppose they don't
think anything of it because, if left unapproached,
they seem to just go on about their business, enjoying their meal and standing around.

Though I have never been lit up in an open field
by the glare of a powerful electric torch, I do belong
to a "herd" that has been spotlighted. Psalm 4:6,
today's verse, unreservedly illuminates those who

belong to God. I find it sobering that the Lord, with all the natural beauty of His universe available to be displayed, would choose to draw the attention of a seeking world to His people. Perhaps He does so because those who long to see something good are wondering if it really is possible, for example, to be deeply glad. They question if anyone can find more happiness than what is produced by their mind-numbing alcohol or drugs. They wonder if it is remotely possible to find true rest when they put their heads on their pillows at night. They doubt that on all of the planet there is a refuge from the constant threat of danger.

These are desires that humans crave. And, rightly so, the best evidence that God is their source for human wishes will be found in others who are experiencing them. For that reason, we who gather with God in His field of provision are going to get the spotlight. The good news is that our job is to go on with what we are enjoying in Him. Like the deer in the field, we don't have to act differently. Just be what we are...partakers of God's goodness. Those who see us will be drawn to our contentment and sense of safety. As they look longingly into our field, may we be careful to invite them in. There's plenty of provision for everyone!

Thank You, Father, for Your bountiful love toward us. I am aware that many in this world desperately hope to see something that yields evidence that Your goodness exists. Some of these people live in ghetto filth, some in war-torn towns. Others live in nice houses in clean neighborhoods where the walls sometimes conceal terrors such as abuse and emotional woundings. Whoever they are, if their eyes turn to me, may they see only the result of a heart that has found delight in You. Make my joy complete. As the peace You give fills me, may it reflect only You when the light shines on me. In Jesus' name. Amen.

11

When God Goes Hunting

He has bent His bow and made it ready.

PSALM 7:12

I've tried to imagine what a deer feels when it suddenly realizes that someone or something is pursuing it. The way its tail flares up and its body crouches in readiness to spring into an escape makes me wonder if it is not only responding to an instinct to survive, but if there is a humanlike fear that grips its mind. Whatever the case may be, deer obviously react to being hunted.

When do humans feel the intense fear of being pursued? Soldiers have certainly felt it. Those who have encountered the evil intentions of a criminal have dealt with it. And some of us have unexpectedly become the hunted when we've faced, for example, the unhappy attitude of a mother bear protecting her cub. While these situations may give way to an adrenaline-drenched terror, there is a time far more serious that generates the absolute worst of emotions.

It is when God goes hunting after an unrepentant heart.

The words of Psalm 7:12-13 would be frightening to read if someone were refusing to yield to God: "If a man does not repent, [God] will sharpen His sword; He has bent His bow and made it ready. He has also prepared for Himself deadly weapons; He makes His arrows fiery shafts." The sobering thought about God's ability to stalk a stubborn soul is that He will surely find it. Realizing this, the only way to avoid His flaming arrows or His finely sharpened sword is to submit in repentance.

The amazing truth is that while "it is a terrifying thing to fall into the hands of the living God," there is a strange comfort in understanding why He comes after us when we balk at repentance. God hunts us because He loves us enough to capture us!

Before God ever nocks an arrow or uses His whetstone to sharpen His sword, it would be wise to kneel on the knees of the heart and submit in repentance. Otherwise, go hide…if you think you can!

O Lord, I know there have been times I would not repent. Yet You came after me because You love me. Thank You! From now on I want to remember that when I fail by sinning against You, running away would be a mistake because You are too good a hunter! Blessed be Your name. Amen.

12

The Drive-Through

Come to Me, all who are weary and
heavy-laden, and I will give you rest.

MATTHEW 11:28

One of the greatest by-products of hunting from a deer stand is sitting still. Even if only for an hour or two, deer hunting can seem like a vacation to a tired soul. One muscle, especially for me, that needs to rest is my brain. My overactive mind can tire me out as quickly as any other part of my body. Far too many nights of sleep have ended prematurely because my mind woke up before my body was ready.

Perhaps you can relate to this embarrassing, but true, story and agree that it is very important to occasionally give the brain a break.

One morning I drove to a town 25 miles from home to take care of some business. I was anxious to get it done so I would have an opportunity to hunt that afternoon. I skipped breakfast at the house and by midmorning I was feeling hunger pangs. Even though I didn't have a minute to spare, I pulled into a fast-food drive-through and placed an order. I was given the total and instructed to pull to the first window. I paid for my food and received about 90 cents in change. I was then directed to the second window.

As I sat at the opening, I could see inside the restaurant. I watched the employees as they slowly lumbered around, talked to each other, laughed, and generally had a merry old time—at the expense of my schedule! I found myself beginning to steam at the sight. I nervously fidgeted with the change I held in the palm of my hand. The swarm of thoughts of all I had yet to do while in town (and all I wanted to say to the manager of the restaurant) began to distort my intelligence. Suddenly, the handful of coins I was palming turned into a payment yet to be made. I thought, *Since I haven't paid and they don't have my money, they're not gonna get any more of my time!* At that, I promptly drove away. I was about two miles down the road before it hit me. My countenance went from a look of mischief to horrible embarrassment. Did I go back? No way! I wasn't about to show my stupid face to that bunch. I fought the hunger. I will admit that a satisfying feeling washed over me when I realized that behind me was a drive-through in total chaos. I could almost hear the window attendant screaming in confusion as angry customers kept saying, "Hey! You numbskull. This is not my order!" I hate to admit it, but I hoped the mix-ups went on for hours.

To say the least, the evening hunt was good therapy for my frazzled brain. I was the better for it. To sit for a while and rest was just what the doctor ordered.

The spirit can gain much benefit from a mind that can find calm. Those who have emotionally worked to exhaustion, who find themselves sitting frustrated in the drive-throughs of life, desperately need a place to retreat. Where can our spirits go to find rest? While a quiet treestand might be a good place for a tired body, it is not the true place of solace for the spirit. Keep in mind that only if the heart leans for a while on the presence of Christ will you find the ultimate comfort. Remember the wisdom of Isaiah 26:3 (NKJV): "You will keep him in perfect peace, whose mind is stayed on You." May today's quiet vigil in your stand be more than just a deer hunt. May it be a time when you can be still and know God.

Dear Lord, I need true rest—not just for my body but for my spirit as well. Thank You for this time You have given me to be quiet. I'm grateful that I can be here with You. Help me to be still and know You are God. In Jesus' name. Amen.

13

The Watch

I will seek the lost, bring back the scattered,
bind up the broken and strengthen the sick.

EZEKIEL 34:16

It only took one episode of leaving home for a hunt
without a wristwatch to teach me a good lesson. I
managed to miss an important meeting because I
didn't head back on time. For that reason, I mounted
a used Timex to my bow. I cut the straps off and
taped the timepiece to the inside of the riser. From
then on, I haven't made the mistake of misjudging
time.

As I was cutting the band of the perfectly good
watch, I thought about what my dad had done years
earlier at our church youth camp. He had been
invited to speak to the youths who had gathered for
a week, and his illustration was brilliant. It was so
moving, in fact, that it is still with me today.

Without any of us knowing it, when Dad
arrived at the camp he stashed a brick, a hammer,
and a screwdriver in the pulpit. In his pocket was a

beautiful, colorful wristwatch. When he was introduced, the first thing he did was pull the watch out
of his coat and ask who would like to have it. Every
hand waved vigorously. Dad picked a young man
and asked him to come forward. As he put out his
hand to take the watch, Dad pulled it back and said,
"Just a second. Before I give this to you, I want to do
something to it."

At that, Dad took out the items he had hidden.
He proceeded to lay the watch on the hard brick,
place the screwdriver blade in the center of the crystal,
and, with a powerful blow of the hammer, hit the
top of the screwdriver handle. Watch parts flew all
over the room! Quickly he gathered up as much as
he could find and piled it into the boy's open hand.
Absolute shock was evident in the young fellow's face
as he returned to his seat with the worthless remains
of what used to be a gorgeous timepiece. The rest of
us sat in stunned silence as Dad taught us about the
sad mistake of unnecessarily destroying our lives
before we give them over to Christ.

Knowing that some of us had already done self-
damage, my dad ended his illustration with the hope
we all needed: "There's no way I can rebuild the
watch my young friend has in his hands; however,
God is able to reconstruct our lives. He even knows

where all the parts are. None of them is lost to Him. He wants to gather them up and restore us to the beauty and usefulness we once held. Do you want Him to do it?"

The altar area filled with young people and tears flowed.

Dad's unforgettable illustration might be what you needed to hear today. If you're wearing a watch, take a look at it. Now is the time to let God begin His repairs. He can make you useful again.

Father in heaven, thank You that I can bring my broken life to You. Sin has scattered me beyond self-repair. Please take the remnants I offer and make me useful again. My time is in Your hands. In Christ's name. Amen.

14

A Select Arrow

He has also made Me a select arrow,
He has hidden Me in His quiver.

Isaiah 49:2

While archery deer season might have its legal limits in terms of the calendar, it lasts 365 days a year for me. This is true because during the off-season I am always tweaking my equipment, trying to improve my advantage against the elusive whitetail. One of the things I enjoy working on is culling my inventory of arrows, keeping only the best for the moment of truth, even though the opportunity may still be months away.

When the season finally arrives, after settling into a deerstand, it is without exception a special moment for me when I remove an arrow from my quiver. Knowing that a second shot might be hard to come by, I am careful to pick an arrow that has a certain mark I have inscribed on its plastic vane: #1. It wears that title because it has been tested and proved it was dependable. To use it is a boost to my confidence level. More importantly, if all goes well in the aiming process, the animal will suffer far less.

I try to fill my quiver with #1s. To go into the woods with less than the best is risky. As a result, there's a strange bond between me and my "aluminum friends." Knowing they had to endure many shots, along with necessary adjustments to have the honor of the hunt, I sincerely value them. Sometimes the corrections even required the heat of a flame in order to get a broadhead to sit aerodynamically true on the tip.

For those who desire to be a straight arrow for Christ, I have a feeling my shaft selection process has a sobering ring of familiarity. The testing, the heat of changing, and the patiently waiting in God's quiver until time to be sent to His target is not easy. For some, it will require slight adjustments. For others, some severe corrections are needed. Though it is a grueling procedure to withstand, the longing to be considered one of His "select arrows" remains.

God wants a quiver full of #1s. Allow Him to do what He must to write on your heart, "a select arrow." May the testing bring a deep joy in knowing He loves you enough to want you to be qualified to fulfill His divine purpose.

Lord, thank You that You have seen the hearts of humankind, yet You still choose to use us. You are the one-and-only Mighty Warrior. It is with an understanding of what is required in order to be one of Your usable arrows that I pray, "Make it so for me." I can now see that the times of testing I have already been through were part of the process. I pray for grace, strength, and mercy to go on with You as You adjust me, correct me, and straighten me to fly true to the places You will send me. In Your name I pray. Amen.

15

A Sound like a Frog

*The memory of the righteous is blessed,
but the name of the wicked will rot.*

PROVERBS 10:7

I climbed onto my ladder stand before daylight and settled in for a morning hunt. There was a sizable pond to my right, and the noises that came from it softly filled the area. One particular sound caught my ear and brought a smile to my face because it reminded me of one of my favorite stories…

A little boy said to his grandpa, "Granddad, make a sound like a frog."

His grandfather was sort of a rough old fellow and bluntly denied his grandson's request. However, the boy was not about to be refused.

"Please, Granddad, make a sound like a frog!"

"No!" came the old man's grouchy reply.

"Oh, please, Granddaddy, make a sound like a frog."

Exasperated with the little guy's persistence, the granddad asked, "Why?"

"'Cause Grandma says, 'When Grandpa croaks, we can all go to Six Flags!'"

It sounds like the grandpa had built a less-than-favorable reputation for himself. His legacy had apparently been established, and the assumption was that he would never change. This story makes me want to work on my memory. By that I don't mean my brain's ability to recall; rather, on how I will be remembered in the minds of others. May it never be that my wife, my children, grandchildren, or friends would ever grimace at the mention of my name.

According to Proverbs 10:7, the key to creating a memory that brings smiles to the faces of those around us is to allow righteousness to reign in our hearts. On the other hand, if we want our names to leave the taste of rottenness in the mouths of those who say them in the future, then all we have to do is embrace wickedness. Things that rot are eventually forgotten completely; they disappear into oblivion. However, Psalm 112:6 honors those who choose God's way with a lasting legacy: "For he will never be shaken; the righteous will be remembered forever."

A good goal for life would be that should the day arrive when we become grandparents, we will never hear any of our grandchildren say, "Granddad, make a sound like a frog."

Lord Jesus, hallowed be Your name. How sweet it is to remember it. Today I place my legacy into Your care. As I pursue Your pleasure, I know one of the benefits will be a sweet remembrance when my name comes to the minds of those who are close to me. Help me end my earthly journey with a reputation that honors both my name and, more importantly, Yours. It's in Your sweet name I pray. Amen.

16

Skin and Ink

Behold, I have inscribed you
on the palms of My hands.

ISAIAH 49:16

As my eyes carefully scan the woods in search of deer, my mind often hums on other matters. Sometimes it may be a business issue I'm working through, a home improvement or repair I'm planning, or something I need to say to someone. Though my body is sitting motionless, my brain is spinning with activity.

On occasion, something of incredible importance may cross my thoughts. I've learned through the years that to be safe, I must immediately write myself a note about it. If I don't, it's lost the moment I go on to something else. One solution that has spared me plenty of trouble has been to scribble my most important memos on the closest surface I can find. During the times when no paper is available, I use the meaty part of my palm as a notepad. That section of the hand seems to receive ink very well, and my critical notes rarely get erased.

This method works great, especially in the tree-stand, for two good reasons. One, slipping a glove down is a lot quieter and requires far less motion than digging through pockets for paper. All I need to retrieve is the pen I conveniently keep in my shirt pocket. Deer are less likely to be spooked by this minimum movement. Second, while a note may be written on paper, I may easily forget to take it out of my camo pants pocket when I get home. However, with an inscription of ink on the skin of my hand, it's at least a 99-percent guarantee that I will eventually see it since my hand rarely leaves my arm! Once home, when I see the note, I immediately recall how important it is and act on it.

Knowing the value I place on what I write on my hand, today's verse provides a great deal of comfort to my heart. What an incredible blessing to think that we are of so great importance to the God of all this universe that He would write us on His hand!

If you are one of those who uses the "skin and ink" method, the next time you are scribbling your thoughts on your epidermis, I hope a warm wave of joy washes over your soul as you recall, "Behold, I have inscribed you on the palms of My hands." In fact, it might even be a good idea for you to write His name on your skin from time to time!

Blessed Father, how grateful I am that You write notes about me on Your palms. To know I am not forgotten is a joy beyond measure. May I never forget You. To Your glory I pray in Christ's name. Amen.

17

The Snort

As for all his adversaries, he snorts at them.

PSALM 10:5

In my 35 years of hunting the whitetail deer, I have had many occasions to be startled by their loud, unexpected snorting. It is especially shocking, for example, before daylight as I slip through the blackness of the predawn hour on my way to a stand. Unaware the deer are there and that my presence in their territory has been detected, I am, without exception, brought to my emotional knees when they make their displeasure known with a resounding nasal blast.

For whatever reason they do it, whether to intimidate a threatening intruder or to warn other deer of danger or to simply clear their "smeller," I am always rattled to the core by the noise. I suppose they are doing what comes naturally, but these sudden, ear-splitting sounds have taken years off my life.

Interestingly, in the Scriptures it is said that man has been known to snort. While the deer does it as an innocent, natural response, man is usually guilty of intentionally using it for an unholy reason. In the original language of Psalm 10:5, the word for snort, *puwach*, has the following connotations: puff, pant, scoff, or speak in a harsh manner. In most cases, it seems that a wicked man's snorting is an audible, outward sign of an inward case of pride and arrogance against the presence of righteousness. Also, it is often a reaction to those times when a person doesn't get his way. Deer likely snort in self-defense. Man, however, snorts in defense of self.

While a deer's snort is distinctively consistent in its sound, man's has various tones to it. It can take the form of a car horn blown by an irate driver. It might come out as profanity when a sore loser is being defeated in a sporting competition. Some snorts sound like malicious gossip intended to demean someone as a result of jealousy. At one time or another you have probably heard a human snort—never a pretty sound to hear or a sweet sound to make.

If we are honest, most of us have been guilty of a forceful, rude blast of pride. Sadly, we have probably done it without knowing what a shock it was to everyone nearby. The next time a startled, vocal deer shocks your socks off, let it remind you to be careful to control your mouth. After all, a snort is just hot air!

Lord, there have been times when I have been considered an enemy to the wicked and have heard their snorts. Thank You for delivering me from the painful effects of their anger. Knowing that scoffing at others is never a sweet sound, I pray that You will come alongside me and help me overcome arrogance in my own heart and avoid blasting others with it. Instead, make my words pleasant to hear in the ears of those around me. In Your name I pray. Amen.

18

Song of the Hunter

*I will sing to the LORD, because
He has dealt bountifully with me.*

PSALM 13:6

One of the advantages of being alone on a deerstand is the opportunity to sing without worrying about hecklers. While the volume might have to be subdued because of the sensitive ears of game, we can deliver a melody and lyrics that never have to be subject to the unsolicited reviews of critics.

One particular type of song that is especially wonderful to sing on the stand is a worship tune. The audience is limited to one, and the Lord will always be impressed with our praise to Him. Psalm 33:1 is an encouraging passage, even for the roughest of voices: "Sing for joy in the LORD, O you righteous ones; praise is becoming to the upright." Even the rugged, untrained voices of the most burly hunters among us bring delight to the Lord. It happens when a song of praise rises from a righteous and grateful soul. No matter what tone is produced, as the vocal cords play the strings of the heart, God is pleased. His concern is "our hearts...not the *Billboard* charts!"

What is a good song for a glad heart to sing? Only the heart of the singer can know. For one, the words may tell of a passage on dry ground through some type of "Red Sea": "He turned the sea into dry land; they passed through the river on foot; there let us rejoice in Him!" (Psalm 66:6). For another, they may sing at the realization of how the sky testifies to the awesomeness of its Maker: "The heavens are telling of the glory of God; and their expanse is declaring the work of His hands" (Psalm 19:1).

Songs with words that are written on grateful tablets of flesh are like snowflakes. No two are alike; each is always an original: "He put a new song in my mouth, a song of praise to our God" (Psalm 40:3).

Whatever your song may be, feel free to sing it in the silence of your deerstand. When you finish, sit quietly and listen—you just might hear the applause of one pair of hands. God will love your singing... that's a promise.

Today I lift my song of praise to You, O heavenly Father. It is one that You put in me. Please accept these words and music from my heart. It is my way of saying thank You for Your boundless love toward me. In Your name I pray. Amen.

19

The Look

*They perish at the rebuke
of Your countenance.*

PSALM 80:16

Have you ever unintentionally wandered under another hunter's stand and ruined his hunt? I hate to admit it, but I've been guilty of that. I'll never forget the expression on the fellow's face when I happened to look up and see him glaring at me. The hunter didn't say anything; he just stared at me in disgust. The look on his unhappy face made me want to find a hole to crawl into.

That wasn't the first time I had been given a look of displeasure. It happened a few times in church when I was growing up. Sometimes as I sat on a pew lined with a bunch of teenagers we would pass notes, whisper, and create a distraction with our giggles.

Up front, in his chair that was elevated and just behind the pulpit, my dad's face would be red with embarrassment that his son was being so unruly. Disregarding how he looked to the congregation who could see him, the preacher would establish a hard-rock look on his face and set his eyes on me. With a stare that would melt cast iron, my dad would wait for me to look his way. Suddenly the blood would drain from my face when I locked eyes with him. There would be absolutely no doubt in my mind that the death sentence for my derriere would be handed down. That's when I would pass the note off to a friend, slither down in my chair, put my hands on my lap, and wait nervously for the last "amen" to be said.

I usually survived those unfortunate episodes, but not without some pain. Today, I'm the better for it. And being a dad myself I have had the chance to use those same discomforting stares on my own kids. If children are sensitive, a parent's facial warnings can be very effective. It worked for my mom and dad, and it's worked for me.

Dads are not the only ones who know how to accomplish something with a piercing facial expression. In today's verse the deplorable state of God's people is described and then the last line of the verse says, "They perish at the rebuke of Your countenance." Does that sound like all God had to do was look at them with displeasure? I have a feeling that when the people realized God saw them as a grievous reproach on His good name, those who cared about their relationship with Him melted with fear.

If we could see His face just once when we bring dishonor to His name, I suspect we would not delay the altering of our ways. The truth is, according to John 16:8, when the Holy Spirit came His work was to "convict the world concerning sin and righteousness and judgment." When our wayward hearts are suddenly pricked by the Spirit of God, we would do well to consider the warning. It is in that moment that the eyes of faith can behold the "rebuke" of God's countenance.

Our heavenly Father loved us enough to accept us the way we were when we came to Him as sinners. However, He loves us enough not to leave us that way. Just as my dad's stern look of vexation toward my misconduct in church was motivated by his care for my character, so is God's look of displeasure for our sinful behaviors an indication that He hopes for a change in our hearts.

Oh, God! My kind Redeemer and Lover of my soul, thank You for caring enough about me to draw me to Yourself. There are times when my

actions must disappoint You. Forgive me, Lord, and cause me to act in such a way that Your face will not scowl but shine with a smile when You look at me. In Jesus' kind name. Amen.

20

What to Wear?

Worship the LORD in holy attire.

PSALM 96:9

Picking the right outfit to wear in public is not one of my better gifts. It is for that reason that my wife, Annie, always has her eye on me as we prepare to leave the house. I can really relate to the comedian who said he was dressed to go out and was standing around waiting for his wife to finish. She walked by him, looked him up and down, and asked with a tone of disgust, "Are you going to wear that tonight?" The only response he could come up with was, "Oh, no, ma'am! I'm just wearin' this while I get ready!"

While I may not be gifted in the area of meeting the public in just the right threads, I believe I have developed the skills required to dress properly for a hunt. (If I approached my dressing for the public with the same effort I put into getting decked out for an archery deer hunt, I could easily end up on the cover of *GQ* magazine. Don't those initials stand for "game quota"?)

Why is clothing an issue in terms of hunting? It's necessary to blend in with the surroundings. Otherwise the highly gifted eyes of a deer can detect a person's presence and his chances for a shot fly out the window of opportunity. If I know, for example, my stand will be in the shadows of heavy, early season foliage, I choose a slightly darker pattern of camo. If more sunshine will be in the woods because the leaves have fallen, I might go the lighter-colored route. Basically, a deer hunter's attire has to be right—and I don't take the responsibility lightly.

Besides the woods, there is another place a hunter can go that requires far greater attention be given to what is worn. What we wear when we call on the name of God and enter into His presence is a very serious matter. Psalm 96:9 specifically lists what should cover us: "holy attire."

What is this holy attire? The righteousness of Christ. To go into the presence of God without it is spiritual disaster. Relying on our own good works leaves us dangerously exposed to God's intolerance of sin. Psalm 5:4 warns, "You are not a God who takes pleasure in wickedness; no evil dwells with You." Nothing good comes from our flesh. It is only corruption. However, thanks to God's provision of a "new self" created in the righteousness of His Son, we can "put Him on" (Ephesians 4:24) and go confidently into God's presence.

Hebrews 10:19-20 encourages us in this way: "Therefore, brethren, since we have confidence to enter the holy place by the blood of Jesus, by a new and living way which He inaugurated for us through the veil, that is, His flesh..." And Isaiah 61:10 is a wonderful comfort: "He has clothed me with garments of salvation, He has wrapped me with a robe of righteousness."

So when we are sitting on a deerstand in our proper attire or in church clothed in our Sunday-best, always remember this: Entry into God's presence is an incredible privilege, and we must be rightly clothed when we get there. Thankfully, Jesus is our attire. "Putting Him on" by faith ensures that when we meet God it is not us that He sees. Instead, it is His Son's righteousness that covers us.

Are you dressed in the right attire?

Blessed be Your name, Jesus, for doing what You did at the cross. May I be found in You, not having a righteousness of my own but only that which is through faith in You. You are blameless,

and I am grateful that You allow weak and sinful people to call You Lord. Please cover me with Your finery. Without it I am doomed. Blessed be Your name. Amen.

21

Prime Time

*In the morning, O LORD, You will hear
my voice; in the morning I will order
my prayer to You and eagerly watch.*

PSALM 5:3

As any deer hunter knows, there's hardly anything more exciting than to finally end the predawn journey to the stand by climbing in, sitting down, and waiting for legal shooting light. No matter how many times it's done, serious outdoorsmen long to do it again.

One thing I love to do after I buckle in, load up, and get my face mask in place is to offer a prayer for the time before me. After that, I put my ears and eyes in search mode. Today's verse reminds me of this process. The psalmist David's routine is perfect for the hunter who rises early. First of all, morning is when we seem fittest for prayer. Our minds are on full alert, we are fresh, and we hopefully have some good rest behind us. Also, we are not yet filled with the business of the day. The morning finds us as mentally uncluttered as we can be. It's a great time—and an important time—to go to the Lord for worship and guidance.

Second, with a clear head that comes with the morning, it is much easier to order our prayers to the Lord. Like well-placed arrows in the hands of a skilled archer, a steady mind can better direct the prayerful petitions of the heart. I am well aware of how spiritually groggy and muddled I can be by the end of a busy day. It's hard to concentrate on anything when the brain is tired and the soul has been beaten by the cares of life. For that reason, an early morning sit in a deerstand is even more important than may be realized.

Finally, David's attitude of "eagerly watching" is worthy of notice. What was he watching for? Knowing that God hates sin, the psalmist vigorously stands guard against entertaining iniquity. His desire to avoid being numbered among the boastful, the liars, the men of bloodshed and deceit drives him to finely tune his senses and start the morning prepared for anything. How well we all would do to follow this order.

If the stand is where you are headed this morning or where you are at this moment, this is prime time for prayer. Take advantage of it!

O Holy God, thank You that I am not alone in these woods. You are here with me, and I am grateful You hear my voice. I know You are a God who takes no pleasure in wickedness. Help me eagerly keep watch against it. Deliver me this day from evil. Lead me in Your righteousness and make Your ways straight before me. I bow my head in reverence to You. Blessed be Your name forever and ever. Amen!

22

Skipping in the Dark

*For I, the LORD your God, will hold your right
hand, saying to you, "Fear not, I will help you."*

ISAIAH 41:13 (NKJV)

There are very few parts of a deer hunt I dislike.
Perhaps the untimely onslaught of gnats that seem
to invade only when a deer is moving toward my
stand would be on the list. (They must love adrena-
line!) The sight of a passing pair of coyotes that
scatters the deer herd leaving me with an early trip
back to my truck is a bummer. These things are ter-
ribly bothersome, but there is another part of hunting
I don't care for at all, even after 35 years in the woods.
It's the early morning treks to the stand by myself in
the pitch-black darkness of the predawn forest.

I'm always grateful when another hunter is along.
Having company puts the joy back into the journey.
Instead of being reduced to a shaky, tentative shuffle
through the forest, the presence of a companion
brings a lilt to my steps. The imagination that would
be hindered by thoughts of a deadly attack by a

cougar, a grizzly, or a bogeyman is freed instead to look forward to the hunt.

There is something familiar about how the presence of a friend squelches the struggle of moving alone through the blackness of the woods. It's the comfort that our heavenly Father gives to those who depend on Him for safety in this world. This is beautifully illustrated in the following poem by Lilah Lehman Gustafson. It is a true story told by a father to his little girl who had brought him comfort years before when he was facing a time of great testing. The verses were read at her father's funeral.

Skipping in the Dark

She trembled with fear as they entered the night
    To shadows like shrouds o'er the land.
She whimpered, "I'm scared of the darkness ahead."
    He said, "Here, my child, hold my hand."
She offered hers up and she clasped it in his,
    Her wee little fist in his palm.
The strength of his grip, and the love in his touch
    To her quiv'ring heart brought a calm.
Her fears now allayed and her courage restored
    She bounced by his side with a lark.
And feeling the grasp of his hand on hers
    She said, "Look! I can skip in the dark!"

Her daddy looked down at his dear little girl,
    So trusting, so sure of his care.
For though she could not see the path in the dark,
    She feared not, for Daddy was there!

The Lord sent a message through his little girl
    That bolstered his own troubled mind.
"I ever am with you; I'll guard every step
    Wherever your pathway may wind.
For I am thy God, I will hold your right hand,
    Fear not, Dear One, I will help thee.
For I am continually here by your side
    Still holding your hand. Trust in Me."

With tears in his eyes, he looked up to the heav'ns;
    The stars gave brightness to night
God prodded his heart, "There's no darkness on earth
    Can ever extinguish the light.
Look up, hurting child, and give me your hand,
    There's light on your pathway so stark.
My hold will not fail, you're secure in my grasp;
    You, too, child, can skip in the dark."

*Dear heavenly Father, thank You for Your confi-
dent hand that reaches for my own. Please let me*

feel the gentle squeeze of it on mine in the dark times of this life. I need Your guidance, Your confidence, and the light of Your love. With these, I too can skip in the night. In Jesus' comforting name I pray. Amen.

23

Little Foxes and Big Toenails

Search me, O God, and know my heart....
See if there is any wicked way in me.

PSALM 139:23,24 (NKJV)

It's the little foxes that spoil the vines" is a familiar quip adapted from Song of Solomon 2:15. There's a ton of wisdom in this ounce of words! From the small, seemingly insignificant irritations that can eventually wreck a marriage to the constant-but-quiet drip of a leaky faucet that becomes a major distraction to our ability to concentrate, the applications are endless.

One important part of our spiritual lives to which "the little foxes" concept should be applied is in the way small sins, if ignored, can lead to accepting greater transgressions. To learn to be faithful in the lesser things is to become a ruler over greater things. The following true (and somewhat gross) story is a prime example from my own experience that illustrates how the Lord used the "little foxes" to alert me to the need to be on guard against even the tiniest of iniquities.

Back in the 70s I traveled with a band. One night, my partner, Ron, and I checked into a Mississippi motel after a concert. As Ron showered before retiring for the night, I took the opportunity to trim my toenails that were long overdue for a pedicure. Instead of placing the trimmings in a wastebasket, I was a slob and threw them at random across the room. My big toe nearly needed a chain saw to remove the unusually long growth. When I finally peeled the ugly thing off, I didn't even look up but just gave it a good fling.

The next morning as I showered, Ron made coffee with the in-room self-service machine. The wall-mounted appliance sat next to a shelf that held glass mugs. I decided to help myself to the brew, so I removed the pot and poured some into one of the cups that rested at eye level on the shelf. After I put the pot back, I began to sip the coffee. I remember making a comment about how good it tasted. Being a good enough blend to be consumed to the last drop, I turned up the cup to consume the remaining portion. That's when I saw it! There in the bottom of the mug was the huge toenail from my big toe that I had pitched the night before. I recognized its shape, but it was now much cleaner than I remembered. I nearly gagged. I was, to say the least, grateful that I'd chosen that cup and not Ron. Ron nearly split a gut when he learned why I was looking so pale.

I suppose I deserved what I got. As I reeled from my self-inflicted nausea, I'll never forget how these words came to my mind: "It's the little foxes…" Strangely enough, I felt a certain guilt for what I had done. I know that toenail tossing does not rank up there with the vilest of sins. While it may have been a small and even insignificant act, it was weighty in its potential. What I was really dealing with was the dangerous intent of my heart.

The evening before, I consciously knew that while I was flinging toenails, I was not doing unto others as I would have them do to me. I showed blatant disrespect for the motel owner, the person who would clean the room, Ron, and the next guest who would occupy the space I was in. (I could only imagine what would have happened had that individual found what I had discovered in the mug. It could have resulted in a nasty confrontation, even a lawsuit!)

As an act of penance, I tried to gather up as much of the toe debris as I could find. I left that motel a different man—perhaps not excelling to the point of sinless perfection, but at least having taken one small step toward righteousness. Oh, how I pray that God always gives me the ammunition of grace to shoot the little foxes!

Lord, thank You for loving me and being patient with me in my struggle to please You. I want to walk worthy of Your presence in my heart. Help me be on guard against the little sins that would come in and try to make my heart an unclean and unwelcome place for Your Spirit to dwell. In Jesus' name I pray. Amen.

24

Safety Belt

He will not allow your foot to slip....
The LORD *is your keeper.*

PSALM 121:3,5

I seriously doubt if any hunter has deliberately jumped out of a treestand for the sole purpose of hurting himself. However, most of us have heard of people who have accidentally fallen and been maimed or even killed. Maybe you have experienced this type of accident (I hope not!). Regretfully, I can testify to the pain of an unplanned fall from a treestand. It's not fun!

Anyone who knows or can imagine how an unexpected plunge feels would never intentionally hurt himself this way. If he did he would have to be crazy! Yet when it comes to injuring our spiritual lives by diving into immorality, mankind can be incredibly dim-witted. Amazingly, lots of folks inflict a "sinjury" to their souls by jumping—not just falling—into transgression.

Consider the wake of painful sorrow that followed

King David after his unholy tryst with Bathsheba (see 2 Samuel 11–12). The consequences he paid were extremely difficult:

> [Thus says the LORD God of Israel,] "Why have you despised the word of the LORD by doing evil in His sight?"...Now therefore, the sword shall never depart from your house, because you have despised Me and have taken the wife of Uriah the Hittite to be your wife...Behold I will raise up evil against you from your own household; I will even take your wives before your eyes and give them to your companion..."The child also that is born to you shall surely die" (2 Samuel 12:9-11,14).

David's situation is fair warning for us all to understand this sobering truth: If a wayward thought is not "taken captive to the obedience of Christ," eventually a decision must and will be made. At some point the chance to sin can turn into a choice to sin. When the resulting pain of the consequences is ignored in advance and our feet leave the platform of holiness, the jump becomes "the fall." When the heart thuds against the hard ground of disobedience, that's when we suddenly realize how stupid we've been.

Smart treestand hunters always use a safety belt, even if they are the most cautious of climbers. I would argue that to consciously avoid using a teth-ering device that could stop a deadly fall is the same thing as deliberately putting yourself in harm's way. This is true because a hunter ascends the tree know-ing the risks involved. The same is true for a person's spiritual walk. To not take advantage of the available safety measures when doing something that is inher-ently dangerous is asking for trouble.

The most modern example I can think of to illustrate this is found on most of our desks in our homes. Climbing into the innumerable branches of the Internet without a filter that blocks the smut sites is a mindless invitation to disaster. Like a belt that makes a hunter safe, an Internet filter protects a sin-sensitive user. The program doesn't falter when our will is weak. With millions of porno websites to log onto, not strapping ourselves to a technical safety device that can effectively assist us with self-discipline is a sad disregard for the deadly dangers.

Are you uncomfortable acknowledging your weaknesses? If so, lean on 2 Corinthians 12:9 for strength: "My grace is sufficient for you, for power is perfected in weakness." To not admit how easy it is to be enticed by ungodly pleasures is the same as leaving your safety belt at home when you go into the tall timber to hunt.

The next time you stand at the bottom of a tree and look up in preparation to climb, remember to ask this probing question that applies to both body and soul: "Where's my safety belt?"

Father, thank You for being my Mighty Protector against a deadly fall into sin. I don't want to be unwise in my climb to heaven. Help me be brave enough to admit that I will always be in need of the safety of Your presence in my life. I know it is foolish to attempt any ascent while I am knowingly disconnected from Your grace. Bless Your name for caring enough about me to remind me of my great need for You. Hang on to me, God. In Jesus' name. Amen.

25

Attacked!

Put on the full armor of God.
EPHESIANS 6:11

M y friend Randy stopped his truck and said,
"This is the place." The North Dakota farm had
numerous good areas for hunting mule deer, and the
one he had chosen was near a river. Before I exited the
vehicle, we agreed on a time he would return to pick
me up. The sun was yet to rise and the warm, August
bow-season morning was already in the low 80s.

As his taillights disappeared into the distance, I
stood in the dark and fastened the four snaps of my
sleeve guard. As I did, I suddenly heard a strange
sound. It was an eerie hum, sort of high pitched and
growing in volume as the seconds passed. I dug for my
flashlight. I didn't want to turn it on and risk alerting
deer that the truck had deposited a human being in
their territory, but I had to find out what the source
of the noise was. When I flicked the light on, what
I saw was unbelievable. I was quickly being covered
by a thick swarm of mosquitoes. Their troops were

innumerable. Realizing I was under serious attack, I immediately abandoned what was to be the first morning of deer hunting in North Dakota and started a brisk walk in the direction of camp. Within 45 minutes the light of the little trailer was in view. When I opened the door, Randy was quite surprised to see me. I was happy to be safely inside and alive.

"I could have died out there!" I blurted. When I explained my dilemma, Randy didn't disagree with my assessment. His only response was, "Are you going back out there?"

"You bet I am, good buddy. I didn't come all the way to North Dakota to be whipped by a few million pesky, pistol-packin' skeeters!" I disappeared into the bedroom, then came out with my "armor" on: two pairs of pants, two shirts, two pair of gloves, and an extra face mask. Of course, in the temperatures of the late-summer plains, the extra clothes made me feel like I was hunting in a sleeping bag inside a sauna. This meant I simply had to make sure the wind was always in my face and I had plenty of water along to replenish my fluids.

The pests swarmed fiercely and made plenty of racket around my ears, but not one of their drills made it through my covering! As I monitored a well-used pass-through area that led from one field to another,

I felt completely safe. The day ended without another single drop of my blood being donated to the bellies of those thirsty creatures. And I managed to bring home a nice mulie. It was some of the best meat I've ever eaten because I won the "war."

Satan also wages a war against us—a spiritual battle that daily challenges the souls who belong to Christ. The enemy and his swarms of schemes would destroy us if we allowed them to. They are constantly on the attack. The good news is that we have protection! There is a suit of armor available to each of us to wear:

> For our struggle is not against flesh and blood, but against the rulers, against the powers, against the world forces of this darkness, against the spiritual forces of wickedness in the heavenly places.
>
> Therefore, take up the full armor of God, so that you will be able to resist in the evil day, and having done everything, to stand firm. Stand firm therefore, having girded your loins with truth, and having put on the breastplate of righteousness, and having shod your feet with the preparation of the gospel of peace; in addition to all, taking up the shield of faith with which you will be able to extinguish all the flaming arrows of the evil one. And take the helmet of salvation, and the

sword of the Spirit, which is the word of God. With all prayer and petition pray at all times in the Spirit, and with this in view, be on the alert with all perseverance and petition for all the saints (Ephesians 6:12-18).

How foolish it would have been for me to go back to the outdoors that morning in North Dakota without the protective covering I wore. Those mosquitoes would have drained me dry in a matter of minutes. It would be just as senseless to attempt to win the war against the devil without proper battle attire. While God's armor might present a little extra weight to carry, we cannot win without it.

Will you suit up?

Father, thank You for providing the equipment I need to fight and win the battle for righteousness. Please guide me to the armor room. Help me don each piece and secure it firmly. I need Your strength to fight and to carry the weight of this suit of armor. Thank You. In Jesus' name. Amen.

26

Whiter Than Snow

Wash me, and I shall be whiter than snow.

PSALM 51:7

Nearly 100 percent of the uncles, aunts, and cousins on the Chapman side of my family have snow-white hair. An in-law once quipped at a Chapman reunion, where the room was full of Chapmans, "This place looks like a big box of Q-tips!" He was right.

I was not spared this trait. As a hunter, my glow-in-the-dark head of hair is a potential hazard. I usually put a mask over my entire head the moment I exit the truck and walk toward my stand, even in the dark of the predawn hour. I'm just sure that a deer's incredible night vision can pick me up as I slip along. In their eyes, without my head covering I would appear to be a mysteriously illuminated globe bobbing by. Even I would be spooked at a sight like that!

Not only do I cover up in order to salvage my deer hunt, I also do it for safety's sake. Since my hair is the same color as some of a deer's fur, like its tail, I rarely remove my mask while I'm in the woods. I wouldn't want a hunter to shoot me and have to check me in at the local hospital.

Though it requires careful attention and constant concealment, in no way do I resent or dislike my "cotton" top. This is true for several reasons. One, I may not be smart but at least I can look like I have the wisdom garnered by time. Two, if I ever get lost in the wilderness, the helicopter pilot can spot me a lot quicker. A third reason to embrace (hold on to!) my frosty flocks is a more recent discovery.

Annie and I were traveling and stopped at a McDonald's restaurant for a quick break and some coffee. I went to the counter and ordered two cups, then met Annie at the car.

"Annie," I announced in amazement, "you wouldn't believe how cheap the coffee is here. I got two cups for 50 cents. Unbelievable!"

As we drove away I noticed Annie looking at me with a silly grin on her face.

"What?" I inquired.

"You have no idea what just happened in there do you?"

"What?" I asked again.

"They gave you the senior discount!" Her laugh was disturbing.

I was appalled at first. I thought about turning around to see if I could get the manager to fire the little snit that undercharged me. However, as I thought about how much savings my new status might represent, I calmed down. So the third reason is appreciating my "seasoned appearance."

The primary reason I am satisfied with my white hair comes back to me when I look in the mirror. Years ago, when I noticed my "pepper" was turning to salt, I found a good way to deal with the impact it was having on my ego. At that time, I was a young Christian and eager to see the Lord in whatever way He would reveal Himself. As the deep-brown hue of my mane began to seriously pale, I decided I could look at it as a constant reminder of how God was kind enough to take my sin-blackened heart, wash it in the red, redeeming blood of Christ, and make it white as snow. It was a transforming decision.

From that era on, I never fought it. I've never had the desire to restore the original color with the liquid youth that comes from a bottle. (Annie said, "Steve, why dye it, it's already died!")

If you are also pigment challenged, count your blessings. Right there on your noggin is the story of the gospel of Christ. Cover it when you deer hunt, but let your light shine when you're not in the woods!

Father, thank You for white hair. Perhaps it is a man's glory not just because it represents the distance he might have traveled in time or the wisdom he has gained, but because it reflects the story of Your love for us. Knowing that You number the hairs on our heads, would You be so kind as to sustain my total? Bless You. Amen.

27

Popsicles

*Each one is tempted when he is carried away
and enticed by his own lust.*

JAMES 1:14

Have you ever been so cold that your fingers and toes became numb? What is especially interesting is how the numbing process is so gradual. As the warm air is slowly replaced by the cold, we sit there oblivious to the change. Then all of a sudden there's a stinging pain. The stiffness makes it hard to regain comfort. We try to wiggle our toes, but they won't move quickly enough. We blow warm air into our gloves to ward off the throb. Usually by then it's too late; the damage has been done.

Many years ago I heard a story about an ancient tribe of Arctic dwellers. They used the numbing effect of ice to destroy the wolves that were coming into their camps and killing their valuable dogs and other animals.

The hunters would coat a knife blade with the fresh blood of an animal, let it freeze, then repeat the same thing over and over until the sharp steel was concealed by a thick covering of frozen blood. Then they would stick it into the ground, handle down and blade exposed upward. When the wolf's well-trained nose would find the enticing, flavorful "Popsicle" trap it would begin to lick it. As the wolf's tongue slowly numbed, the smell of the blood drove him to keep licking. By the time it licked down to the finely sharpened blade, its tongue would be so deadened by the ice that the wolf didn't know the blade was slicing its tongue to shreds. Wounded, the predator would wander away and likely starve to death.

While this method of hunting is unusually cruel, it is effective. The way intense cold sneaks up and wreaks havoc is a good picture of a spiritual truth. Through habitual sin, the "skin of our spirit," can be numbed, which eventually can block our ability to feel the "godly sorrow that leads us to repentance" (2 Corinthians 7:10). How many of us have given in to sordid hungers and were slowly numbed by them, so much so that we kept consuming until our "tongues" reached the blade of destruction—and sometimes continued until death.

Why don't you stop for a moment in this bitterly cold world we live in and carefully consider what you are consuming? Are you licking with a frenzy on any

"Popsicles"? If so, ask God to help you now and renew your sensitivity to His leading.

O Lord, I'm grateful that You can help me avoid being numbed by sin. Deliver me today from the trap of Satan's enticements. I pray for Your wisdom and strength to be able to see them and flee from them. Please hear my cry. Thank You. In Jesus' name. Amen.

28

The Trail

That the generation to come might know,
even the children yet to be born, that they
may arise and tell them to their children.

PSALM 78:6

I had cleared the trail to one of my favorite stand locations two years earlier, and it was time to do it again. Restoring it to a path that would ensure a quiet, undetected walk to the tree I would use required a rake for the layers of leaves that had fallen. Also, some trimming of the new growth of overhanging branches was necessary. After about an hour, I was standing under the familiar tree that held the sturdy platform. I carefully checked each step as I ascended and climbed in for a moment's rest.

It was quiet except for the mid-August mosquito buzzing at my ear. I surveyed the shooting lanes around the stand. They needed a little work too. Before climbing down to complete the job, I looked over the trail that snaked off into the woods. I was satisfied it was ready for the upcoming season.

This trail had some good memories attached to it. I replayed the scene when a buck that had eluded me on several occasions came within 20 yards of my stand. The crunch of the leaves that alerted me to his presence echoed in my head. I could almost feel the slight sting of the kisser button sliding across my lower lip as the string was released. The snap of the bow limbs and the crashing sound as he ran off came rushing in. I could even feel the deep, nervous sigh that followed the shot. I recalled how it seemed to take minutes before I could exhale. It was an incredible moment. Isn't it great how memories can bring joy to our hearts?

As I climbed down and headed to my truck, I thought of my freshly cleared trail. Back there was a stand that was not just a platform at a "honey hole." It was a monument that honored the wonderful memories of seasons passed. I couldn't wait for the first day of season when I could follow my homemade path back to that special spot.

Trails are that way. They lead to destinations we long for and places we enjoy going back to. Besides my treestand trail, there's another one I love to travel: the trail that winds through time on my way to heaven. There's an awesome destination waiting for every believer! But there are places on this trail that I love to wander back to. The spot that means the most to me is best described in this lyric about my grandfather.

One Man Prayed

Back behind me on the trail of time
There is a place that is sacred to me
Sometimes I go there in my mind
And I look upon it thankfully.

'Cause it was there long before my years
That a man whose blood runs through my veins
Fell on his knees and he said with tears
"God save my soul in Jesus' name."

That was the place, that was the time
When amazing grace came into my bloodline
And my soul was forever changed
When one man prayed in Jesus' name.

If time goes on further down the trail
Others will be born, and born again
And if I'm around I'll be sure to tell
How it came to pass that grace came in.

That was the place, that was the time
When amazing grace came into my bloodline
And so many souls were forever changed
'Cause one man prayed in Jesus' name.

Take a moment and think about your life. Where is your path taking you? What has happened behind you that means the most? Consider the things you do and how they will affect those who come down the trail behind you.

Lord, thank You and bless You for meeting my ancestors on this trail through time. I'll be forever grateful that the choice they made for You not only changed their lives but mine as well. Help me to be careful in my heart to keep on this way to heaven, especially for the sake of those who follow. And until I get home to be with You, I need the light of Your love to guide me. In Jesus' name. Amen.

29

Apple Seeds

*The earth brought forth vegetation,
plants yielding seed after their kind, and trees
bearing fruit with seed in them, after their kind;
and God saw that it was good.*

GENESIS 1:12

Whenever snacktime arrives while sitting in a deerstand, one of the best treats a hunter can take out of his pack is a fresh apple. The natural sugar is a boost, and the unique taste can wake the sleepiest of heads. Also, the aroma could very well get the attention of the sensitive nose of a hungry deer, enticing it into range.

Because this fruit is a familiar food to whitetails in this part of the country, I usually don't consume the entire apple. Instead, I save enough on the core to ensure it has plenty of pulp to give off a pleasing odor. I then put it under my boot and quietly smash it. Using the grated floor of the stand, I let the sweet-smelling debris fall through it to the earth below.

Whenever I crush an apple this way, I know that

along with the ground-up meat of the fruit, the seeds fall to the soil as well. I've wondered if someday, years in the future, others will be able to track my stand locations by finding apple trees that have grown up in nondescript places in the middle of the woods!

If my stand has a solid floor, I do something a little different. Before consuming the apple, I take out my pocketknife and slice it in half. I'll eat one side and cut up the rest in small pieces and toss them out around me. Sometimes before I partake, I look at the nicely sliced halves and observe the exposed seeds. I like to do this because of a profound quip I heard several years ago: "You can count the seeds in an apple, but you can't count the apples in a seed."

An amazing amount of truth is packed into these few words. I find them especially inspiring when the opportunity arises to share the good news of the gospel of Christ with a group of young people. To think that even though I may be speaking to a few individuals who can be quickly counted, they in turn could bear spiritual fruit and possibly affect many others through the years. Sunday school teachers and camp counselors, for example, will be encouraged if they remember this truth when they get weary in well doing.

The potential of divine multiplication is even more heartening when I consider the fact that in my own home there once were two youngsters. They are now grown and on their own, but while they were with us Annie and I were careful to present Christ to them. It was truly exciting when each one of them confessed Jesus as Lord and Savior. While they are "just two," there's no way to calculate the eventual influence their testimonies might have on other people.

If you have an apple with you, open it up. Take a look at the little black dots inside. Count them. Remember, you are holding not just one seed but many apples that could feed many people and animals. Who could number them? The final tally is known only to God. Keep this in mind the next time the opportunity comes to share the good news of Jesus!

Father in heaven and maker of the apple trees and seeds, thank You for the way a seed can carry so much life. I pray for Your courage to seize every opportunity to share the gospel of Your Son. Though my audience may be small

and quickly numbered, You can use them to reach others with Your love. Yours is the only love that deserves to go on through time. In Jesus' name. Amen.

30

Words

*Every careless word that people speak, they shall
give an accounting for it in the day of judgment.*

MATTHEW 12:36

Another Friday came and it was time for the
Chapmans to travel again. Though I would have
enjoyed a trip to the woods for a leisurely hunt, I went
along with the idea of having a job as we loaded the
van and headed to the airport.

The call to board was made, and we took our
seats toward the front of the cabin and settled in. I
was next to the window, Annie was in the middle,
and the kids occupied the aisle seats. Suddenly
Annie nudged me gently in the ribs and gave me that
Quick! Look-over-my-shoulder-at-something-important
nod. When I leaned my head around to take a peek,
I was visibly taken aback.

Standing in the aisle right between Nathan and
Heidi, waiting for other passengers to fill the overhead bins with their stuff, was a musician we had
only seen on TV. If I gave the name most would

know it. He (that narrows it down) was a highly flamboyant artist, and his fame was well established in the marketplace. I nearly gasped at how striking he looked in his dark, long, flowing overcoat. The sunglasses were quite impressive. And the ring on his hand must have weighed in at a hefty 12 pounds. It sparkled like a spider web in the bright morning sun.

Annie and I didn't bring him to the attention of our children. Nathan was about ten and Heidi was around seven. We knew they would know who he was. We also knew that they had seen and heard our comical comments and expressions about him whenever he was gracing our TV set. To avoid their excited chatter, we both held our breath as the man passed.

What happened next was totally unexpected. Before they closed the door of the plane, Annie got a tap on the shoulder. It was the well-dressed woman who had followed the celebrity onboard.

"Hi! I'm _____, _____'s wife, and he would like to meet the two of you."

Needless to say, we were completely bewildered that he would remotely know who we were. Both of us felt totally unprepared, but to be nice we complied. In the mental chaos of the moment we forgot how we had acted when we had seen this man on TV in the secrecy of our den. We asked, "Nathan, Heidi, do you want to go with us?" Little did we know that we had just invited trouble to accompany us to the back of the cabin.

As we were being quite properly introduced, Nathan's eyes got bigger than fried eggs. I could tell he wanted to say something, but my brain couldn't register what it might be. When it came his turn to shake the hand with the diamond-studded ring, Nathan spoke up in a voice that filled the airplane up to ten aisles away on both sides. "Oh! Mom and Dad! Isn't this the guy you always make fun of?"

Needless to say, I wanted to crawl into the overhead bins above me. No, better yet, I wanted the rapture to happen! I could feel my knees grow weak, and my pulse begin to falter. Annie sort of jerked as if she had been hit with a stun gun. It was awful. Annie is much "quicker on her feet" than I am. As Nathan's query dangled in the air like a wrecking ball, she made a valiant attempt to salvage our reputation. "Don't kids say the darndest things? He's just being silly." She and I both knew it wasn't Nathan who looked silly. We were caught red-tongued. Oh, how it hurt.

I'm not sure if he (the artist) or we (the dummies)

ever fully recovered from that encounter. One thing is for sure, we learned two huge lessons that day. One, if you don't want it repeated, don't say it in front of kids. And two, it would always be smart to obey the instructions given in Ephesians 4:29. They are there not just to fill space on a page but for the good of us all. To heed them could spare a soul from a lot of grief!

> Let no unwholesome word proceed from your mouth, but only such a word as is good for edification according to the need of the moment, so that it will give grace to those who hear.

Forgive my mouth, Father, for sometimes I use it before engaging my brain! In Jesus' name. Amen.

31

And So They Prayed

*Devote yourselves to prayer, keeping alert
in it with an attitude of thanksgiving.*

COLOSSIANS 4:2

Whenever I deer hunt with my muzzle loader, I usually think about the story in the following lyric. It's a ballad set in the era of the Civil War.

And So They Prayed

A young golden-haired soldier stood in the ranks of the
    brave
And the captain said, "Guns to the shoulder!"…and they
    quietly marched away.

His blue eyes once thrilled his mother, but now they
    were filled with fear
As he heard the cannon's thunder and the field of the
    battle drew near.

But in that moment, far away, a mother whispers,
    "Amen."

'Cause she thought of her son and so she prayed, and
O how she prayed for him.

His young hands, once they were steady, when he'd
hunt by his father's side
But now they trembled as he readied his gun, and the
enemy came into sight.

But in that moment far away, a father whispers, "Amen."
'Cause he thought of his son and so he prayed, and O
how he prayed for him.

How quickly his legs once carried him, when he'd run
with his sister to town
But he could not run from the bullet within, and so he fell
to the ground.

But in that moment far away, a sister says, "Amen."
'Cause she thought of her brother, and so she prayed,
and O how she prayed for him.

Well the letter arrived, it was stained with blood, and it
was sadly received
And gathering around were the ones he loved, and they
began to read.

But in that moment far away, a young soldier whispers,
"Amen."

'Cause he thought of his family who would hear of his
    wounds, and so he prayed for them

O how he prayed for them
'Cause he knew they must have been praying for him.

Besides making an attempt to capture the emotions a soldier might face during the horrors of battle, I had an alternative motive in telling this story. I was taught by my parents to always be alert to those moments when a loved one comes to mind unexpectedly. To ignore the sudden thoughts might mean overlooking the move of the Holy Spirit to pray for that person. That's what the family in the song did for the soldier, and that's what I want to do as well.

Perhaps you have never considered using unanticipated thoughts of your loved ones as a cue to pray for them. All kinds of wars are being waged in the hearts of humans. A child at school, a spouse at home or at work, or a friend in a faraway place might be facing a spiritual battle. Is it beyond God's ability to move one person to pray for another? Certainly not! Today as you hunt, be on the alert for God bringing someone to mind whom you can lift up in prayer.

Lord, thank You for helping me be attentive to Your Holy Spirit. If there is one soul I can especially pray for today, please bring his or her name to my heart. Help me be a faithful watchman for the signal to lift a loved one to You. In Jesus' name. Amen.

32

Fall Blend

A time to plant...

ECCLESIASTES 3:2

I felt a little strange as I sowed the highly palat-
able mix of deer-friendly forages in the middle of
August. It didn't feel right. Being a latecomer to the
science of farming, I held a preconceived notion that
the time to plant was only in springtime. But the
seeds I was broadcasting were specifically developed
for autumn growth. Still, it was hard to believe the
message on the label of the two-and-half-pound bag:
"Fall blend: best results if sown from mid-August to
mid-September."

The instructions on that sack of seed was a pleasant but puzzling discovery for this new farmer. To
be sure of the facts, I asked my expert-gardener wife,
Annie, if this was normal. She informed me that certain flowers, such as tulips, mums, and her favorite,
the hyacinth, can safely and effectively be planted
after summer has passed. My perception about

springtime and harvest was delightfully changed, and I gladly accepted the exceptions to the rules.

There's a certain comfort that can be drawn from this truth about autumn planting. And it's a consolation not just for the hunter who wants to create a tasty food plot to entice wary deer into range, but also for newly converted parents who have grown children. Only recently did I notice that a season is not mentioned in today's well-known verse, only "a time" to plant. As a result of coming to Christ later in years, the opportunity parents had to sow the seeds of the Scriptures into their children's hearts when they were young might have passed. With children who are beyond the springtime of their lives, to understand that fall planting is perfectly fine is great solace.

It wasn't until his later years that Paul, the apostle, was drastically changed from a persecutor of the saints to a champion of the cause of Christ. Moses was chosen in his fortieth year to lead God's people. Zacchaeus, the tax collector, met with salvation as an adult when he encountered the compassionate Christ. Somewhere in the hearts of these men were the divinely prepared soft spots where a seed could be sown. The same is true for adults today. Whether you are a mom or dad who is a latecomer to the kingdom of God or a longtime believer, there is hope since it is never too late for planting. May God bless you as you open your container of seed (the Scriptures) and seize the opportunity to sow into the hearts of your eye-level children in any season.

O, God! I have missed the spring season of sowing Your Word into my children's hearts. How grateful I am that it can also be done in the fall. I pray for opportunities to plant You in their lives. I trust You to soften the ground in their souls to receive You. In Jesus' name. Amen.

33

Pick a Spot

Forgetting what lies behind and reaching
forward to what lies ahead...
PHILIPPIANS 3:13

My new, whisper-quiet recurve worked beautifully as I came to full draw and released a cedar shaft arrow at the heavy doe below me. Unfortunately, my brain wasn't working as well as my bow. The arrow flew over the deer's back. So did the second shot. The third dug into the ground under her belly, and the fourth sailed to who knows where.

I couldn't believe it. Four golden opportunities royally blown. As the deer wandered off and left me bleeding profusely from the wounds in my ego, I began to mentally replay the misses to determine what I had done wrong. It didn't take but a minute of pondering my poor performance to come up with the answer. Without a doubt, I had allowed the presence of a real deer to get the best of me. As a result, I committed a fatal error. I failed to *pick a spot*. Instead of honing in on a tuft of hair or a shadow behind the deer's shoulder blade, I let the animal become a sil-houette. Consequently, I left the tree with an empty quiver and a tag that would not be filled.

As disgusting and frustrating as failures can be, there's always something to learn from them. This bungled opportunity was no different. My inability to key in on a specific target on the deer's body was a product of forsaking the basics. That error can be corrected with experience; however, the other reason I squandered the chance for success will be much harder to overcome. And to tell you what that is requires a confession.

I was yet to score with traditional equipment. I consider it one of a deer hunter's greatest challenges. So to put it simply, I wanted to be able to brag to my wife, my hunting buddies, and to all who would hear me gloat, "I did it! Me! Me! I got a recurve kill!" I was so wrapped up in being able to tout success that I couldn't hold on to the rudiments of taking a shot. My ability to focus was destroyed by my pride. I had no plans for humility; as a result, humility is what I got.

How often in the rest of life do we face this same dilemma? For example, in an effort to impress their business partners some people forget the foundational principles of good ethics. Shots that completely miss the mark of good morals include shady deals and under-the-table trades for the sake of bolstering the bottom line.

In Philippians 3, the apostle Paul gives us the best advice regarding how to hone in on a specific target. It works for bowhunters *and* believers. First, "forgetting what lies behind": ignoring, as Paul did, the reputation of previous successes. He abandoned the desire to protect the pride that accompanies accomplishment. Second, he "reached forward to what lies ahead": in the same way a traditional shooter points his extended arm at the target, Paul directed his gaze to obeying Christ. With his eyes fixed on Jesus alone, he found his "spot" (see Hebrews 12:2).

I can't wait until next archery season to try my recurve again. Until then, I have to work on my skills as a shooter and the attitude of my heart. My plan is to adopt Paul's fine example for hitting the target: *Forget* and *reach*. I have a feeling it's going to work!

Lord, bless You for being longsuffering with me.
Too often I have focused on the wrong things.
Help me concentrate on obedience, not success.

Help me keep the basics before me. And until I am safe with You, I will continually aim for the mark of being Christ-minded. In Jesus' name. Amen.

34

He Never Did Anything

They shouted back, "Crucify Him!" But Pilate said to them, "Why, what evil has He done?" But they shouted all the more, "Crucify Him!"

MARK 15:13,14

Two years ago I had the unforgettable opportunity of singing in a midwestern prison. I'll never forget the strange feelings I had when I entered the facility with the chaplain and the doors slid back into their secure, locked positions behind us. It was lunchtime, and the halls were filled with men who moved in an orderly fashion toward the eating area. Some smiled, some said hello, and others looked quite somber as they passed. I cannot imagine being confined in the way these men were. Being an avid outdoorsman, I think if I were locked up I would probably wear one of those expressionless faces when I passed visitors in the hall.

Sometimes when I'm headed down the open highway on a drive to hunt or sitting in the quiet of a treestand looking out through the wild of the woods, I think of those men. I can see the faces of the ones who sat on the first row of the pews in the chapel. How many of the guys that filled the room that day would give nearly anything to be in the freedom of my boots? All of them. When they come to mind, I pray for them.

I can recall the chaplain's description of how one particular thing kept many of the inmates emotionally strong. It was their intense hope that their innocence would soon be confirmed and result in their release. He relayed how so many of the men would dive headlong into studies of the law in order to find a loophole or legal precedent that would work in their favor.

When a man is behind bars and is convinced of his innocence, the sorrow must run even deeper. It would take a man like this to better understand the injustice served to Christ as Pilate handed down the sentence of death to the Savior. One such gentleman, a prisoner in the state of Ohio, came to grips with how Jesus must have felt. James Alley maintains that he was accused, tried, convicted, and punished for doing nothing. As an inmate, James prays that someday his case will be retried with fairness. But he's not just a prisoner; James is also a talented lyricist.

One day I was privileged to receive one of his songs in the mail. When I learned about his situation, the following lyric became even more meaningful. As you read it, see if you can feel James' emotion as he closely relates to his Savior.

He Never Did Anything

There's an angry crowd outside the city walls
And they're cursing at a man hanging on a cross
They're saying to Him, "Save Yourself if You're a king!"
But He was blameless as a lamb, He never did anything

Chorus
He never did anything but come to save the lost
He never did anything but pay the final cost
He healed the sick, raised the dead, and took away the
      sting
But when it came to finding fault in Him, He never did
      anything

When there's an angry storm that grows inside of me
I put my trust in the One who calmed the angry sea
And when I'm lonely He makes my sad heart sing
How could they ever crucify Him, He never did anything

Although your flesh is enjoying the freedom of your deerstand and the open spaces of the great outdoors, do you feel "locked up" in your soul? Perhaps it's because you have been wrongly accused of something and you feel bound by the injustice. Or is there some other emotion that makes you feel like a prisoner? If so, take this opportunity to appreciate what Christ went through for you. My favorite part of James' candid lyric is his readiness to take his loneliness and sorrow to the one who was killed in spite of His innocence. Let James' example remind you to go to Christ in prayer with your gratitude for the sacrifice of His innocence for your sins. If you will, the storm might subside, and your joy may return.

Bless You, Father, for the freedom I have to bring my burden of bondage to You. As I cast my cares upon You, deliver me from my accusers. And until I am released from this injustice, I will trust You to be my most treasured companion in this place. In the name of Your innocent Son I come to You. Amen.

35

Twice Amazed

Now when Jesus heard this, He marveled.
MATTHEW 8:10

The incredible sights of nature often leave me speechless. From incredible sunrises and brilliant white stars that dance in the night skies to uniquely colored patterns on butterfly wings and shades of gray fog over quiet ponds, I have had many opportunities to feel the sensation of wonder. I love those moments.

As much emotional depth and height that the sensation of awe holds for us who observe nature, it seems reasonable to assume that Jesus would have felt constantly amazed. After all, He is the Son of the one and only God who created all that intrigues us. However, in a Sunday sermon by Pastor Bill Rudd from Michigan, he noted that in all of the Gospels it is said that Jesus was only twice amazed. And in both instances it had nothing to do with the natural wonders of the universe. Instead, it had only to do with the human heart in relation to faith.

In Matthew 8, the centurion came to Jesus and requested that He heal his paralyzed servant. Feeling totally undeserving that Christ would enter his home, the centurion said in verses 8 and 9:

> Lord, I am not worthy for You to come under my roof, but just say the word, and my servant will be healed. For I also am a man under authority, with soldiers under me; and I say to this one, "Go!" and he goes, and to another, "Come!" and he comes, and to my slave, "Do this!" and he does it.

It was following the centurion's stated understanding of Jesus' ultimate authority, that Jesus marveled.

The second recording that shows Jesus' amazement is found in Mark 6, when Jesus was in His hometown. The people were astonished by His teaching, yet they questioned His wisdom and His miracles. They said, "Is not this the carpenter, the son of Mary, and brother of James and Joses and Judas and Simon? Are not His sisters here with us?" As a result, it is noted in verse 5: "And He could do no miracle there except that He laid His hands on a few sick people and healed them." In verse 6 it is revealed, "And He wondered at their unbelief."

In these two cases it was both the great amount of faith and the lack of it that caused Christ to express

His amazement. The two extremes got His divine attention.

Do you understand and embrace the absolute authority of the risen Christ and His ability to command all that is seen and unseen? Meditate on Jesus' wisdom and miraculous, healing touch.

O amazing Jesus, I come in Your name. I am awed by Your great wisdom, Your unparalleled authority, and the miracle of redemption You so lovingly supplied at the cross. I bow my heart before You and, with trembling flesh at the very thought of it, I look forward to the day I can behold Your face. Until then, may You always make me worthy of Your presence in my heart. Amen.

36

Straight to the Pantry

Enter His gates with thanksgiving and His courts
with praise. Give thanks to Him, bless His name.

PSALM 100:4

There's a certain etiquette that is appropriate for
deer hunters to follow when using property that
belongs to a resident owner. If we go on the land in
the waking hours, it is best to not go directly to the
deerstand. Instead, it is a courtesy to take the time to
stop and greet the owner if he or she is at home and
available for a brief visit. This allows you the opportunity to offer a word of thanks for the privilege to
hunt and alert the owner to your specific whereabouts,
which will ensure his good graces.

How rude it would be to always go through the
gates of the farm, blast by the landowner with a
hurried wave, and go straight to the "goodies" the
property offers. It would be akin to a dinner guest
knocking on your door and, after you open it, ignoring you, brushing by you, and going directly to your
table. There he proceeds to help himself to your

hard-earned, carefully prepared food. Wouldn't you feel unappreciated? Sure you would.

There's a picture in this for those of us who go to the Lord in prayer. So many times we open up with, "Our Father in heaven." Those words are the knock at His door. If our very next words include statements such as, "do this" or "do that," then for all intents and purposes we have walked by the Master of the house and, as someone once quipped, "gone straight to His pantry."

On the other hand, to follow our opener with the courtesies noted in today's verse means we have properly come into His presence.

"Enter His gates with thanksgiving." That alone could keep us at God's door for the rest of our days. Because He has granted us untold blessings for which to be grateful, to try to express them all each time we pray would be impossible. Instead, we can take a few moments to list several of His blessings that are currently on our hearts.

One of the instances when I can be guilty of improper entry into God's presence is at the supper table. It is such a brief visit and more often than not the prayer is handled with less than the best of care. Too many times it sounds like, "Dear Lord, bless this food we are about to receive. Amen!" With very little effort and extra time the prayer could be improved: "Dear Lord, thank You for Your abundant provision. You are our kind God, and we appreciate Your care for us." With something similar to that as the opener, I have then followed the example of "entering His gates with thanksgiving."

The second phase is to "enter His courts with praise." In the same way a hunter compliments a farmer for his kindness and the beauty of his property, one who goes to the Lord can applaud His attributes. Honoring His majesty, glory, omnipotence, and any other divine qualities that our hearts are aware of reveals our respectful hearts.

There are always exceptions to the rules, of course. There will be situations, such as (gulp!) falling out of a treestand, when we must cry out for help and mercy. In that moment, our hearts instantly recognize God's great abilities and His kind willingness to deliver us. Going to Him first is in itself a high compliment to His power. But to always pray in this way is something we should work to change.

By remembering to make the effort to not go directly to the deerstand on someone else's property, we can be reminded to not go to God's house and make the discourteous mistake of going straight to His pantry!

O Lord, I know I need to enter into Your holy presence in the proper manner. Thank You for Your kindness and patience in giving me an example to follow. "Our Father who is in heaven, hallowed be Your name. Your kingdom come. Your will be done, on earth as it is in heaven. Give us this day our daily bread. And forgive us our debts, as we also have forgiven our debtors. And do not lead us into temptation, but deliver us from evil. For Yours is the kingdom and the power and the glory forever." Amen.

37

He Can, Can He?

All things are possible to him who believes.

MARK 9:23

A funny thing happens in my head when a buck is coming toward my stand. If the deer's approach is slow, giving me time to mull over the shot, my mind bounces back and forth, sounding as if I'm talking about another person: "Can he make the shot?" "He can." "Can he?" One reveals confidence; the other shows doubt.

I would almost rather a deer surprise me with a sudden appearance so I can react with the skills I have developed. But more often than not, I end up in the mental tug of war between *can* and *can't*. Fortunately, *can* has won the skirmish most times.

This struggle between "he can" and "can he?" has a familiar ring. In the Gospels of Matthew and Mark, two perceptions of Christ are recorded. They represent an incredibly important application. In Matthew 8:2 it is said, "And a leper came to Him and bowed down before Him, and said, 'Lord, if You are willing, You can make me clean.' " The terminally ill man didn't indicate any doubt in Christ's ability to heal. He only asked if Jesus was willing. The result was a cleansing from his leprosy.

The opposite attitude is found in Mark 9:22. A father had brought his demon-possessed son to Jesus. Since childhood the boy had torturous episodes of convulsing, falling to the ground, and rolling about while foaming at the mouth. Sadly, the father revealed a heart lacking belief when he said, "If You can do anything, take pity on us and help us!"

Jesus must have noticed the word *if.* His response was an indictment of the father's shortness of faith. I imagine it might have been with raised eyebrows that Christ showed His surprise and said, "'If You can?' All things are possible to him who believes." Feeling the sting of the tone of Jesus' words, the desperate father immediately had a change of heart and cried, "I do believe; help my unbelief." His son received deliverance.

Although the outcome was glorious in both cases, the father of the demon-possessed son had much to learn from his lack of faith. Like him, our own faith seems to falter at times. It is an awesome moment when doubt gives way to confidence in Christ's ability to perform the miraculous. This flip-flop that takes us from defeat to victory is a work of the Holy Spirit in our lives. It happens when we suddenly realize whom we are addressing.

The next time a bruiser buck makes your brain swing between confidence and doubt, may it remind you of a struggle and response that reaches beyond a trophy kill: "All things are possible to him who believes."

Blessed Father, thank You for Your patience when I stumble. May Your Holy Spirit continue to remind me of who I am addressing when I come to You with my needs. Draw me close, Father, and forgive me for my lack of faith. In Jesus' name. Amen.

38

Thanks, Adam!

Then to Adam He said, "Because you have
listened to the voice of your wife, and have
eaten from the tree about which I com-
manded you, saying 'You shall not eat from
it'; cursed is the ground because of you...Both
thorns and thistles it shall grow for you."

GENESIS 3:17,18

People tell me I'm a reasonably patient fellow who is generally not too quick to fly off the handle. They say it takes quite a lot to rattle me. These kind folks, however, have yet to be near me when I'm in a brier thicket tracking an arrowed deer. They haven't observed me when every step is being thwarted by relentless, spiny claws. I can't stand them!

As the thousands of tiny spears that line the tangled branches tear at my clothes and turn them into shredded cotton, I quickly change from a mild-mannered soul to a tooth-grinding grumbler. And the vocalization of my anger is not usually subdued—it is audible and delivered with abandon.

When the briers rip at my costly camo and my flesh, it is tempting to use some "colorful" words. I am aware of the need to maintain a certain level of integrity, so I make a concerted effort to limit my verbiage to a form of righteous indignation. It's not an easy task, but I do my best.

Of all the things I can say about the thorns that fight my every move, there are two words, when spoken out loud, that seem to be good therapy for my rage. These noncurse words usually come when I have to repeatedly remove my hat and gloves off branches that have grabbed them. They are: *"Thanks, Adam!"*

When I resort to this phrase, I am not casting blame. I am simply recognizing that the mess I am trying to plow through is literally a product of the original sin of Adam. When he disobeyed God and the ground was cursed, little did he know that his choice would be felt by a lone hunter far into the future—outside the Garden, across the great waters, in a land called America, in a state called Tennessee. And Adam couldn't have known that his name would fall so resentfully from that hunter's lips. But far worse than this, Adam didn't know that the day would come when thorns, one of earth's most annoying evidences of mankind's sin of transgression, would be cruelly used in mockery to crown the innocent one as He died on the cross. (Remember this the next time the thorns draw your blood!)

If there is one thing good that a battle with a brier patch can yield, it is the reminder that I have two children who may someday have children, who in turn may bear offspring. In the same way that Adam's choice to sin affected my life (in more ways than just torn camo), what I do today could cause others in the future to experience unneeded entanglements. May their future never find them stuck woefully in the middle of emotional or spiritual thorns as a result of my disobedience. And may it never come to pass that any of them would angrily say, "Thanks, Dad!" or "Thanks, Grandpa!" The thought that my name would ever be uttered with the slightest tone of disgust is too sad to ponder. That very idea motivates me to live righteously.

None of us is going to be a perfect ancestor. Through careful obedience and a daily pursuit of Christlikeness, we can avoid being dishonored in the years ahead by unwise decisions made today.

Allow God to clear the ugly brier bushes in your heart because, someday, others will be dealing with the path you followed.

Dear Lord, thank You for listening to my heart today. Your mighty hand to deliver me from being a source of thorns in another person's life is something I need. Clear away the unholy growth in the soil of my flesh. I trust You to make the ground of time passable for those who come behind me. In Jesus' name I humbly ask this. Amen.

39

Bottle and Book

You have taken account of my wanderings; put my
tears in Your bottle. Are they not in Your book?

PSALM 56:8

Two of the most important items in my day pack
that goes with me to the deerstand are my water
bottle and my little book of Scriptures. Both items
meet a specific thirst. The water is especially important if I make a shot and have to spend significant
time and serious energy tracking an animal. This is
especially crucial in the early, warmer parts of the
archery season here in Tennessee.

The Bible is a blessing to a thirsty soul. The con-
tents quench the need to not let a day pass without
hearing from the God who loves both our bodies and
souls. The thirst in my spirit is something the flesh
often fights. Though it tries to keep me from drink-
ing from the Bible's pages, I know to ignore God's
Word will leave me dry in my heart.

As I was in the woods taking in God's Word one
day, I saw something interesting in light of what I carry

in my day pack. God, too, has a bottle and a book. Today's verse references this and tells us He stores something very special in those items. They don't contain a source for His longings or something to satisfy a need. Instead, they hold the record of those times we desperately thirsted for Him. Our tears of affliction are kept in His divine container as well as on the stained pages of the journal He keeps of our lives.

God has preserved the tears of Job, the countless captives, the oppressed, Jeremiah, and the widow of Nain (see Job 16:20; Psalm 126:5; Ecclesiastes 4:1; Jeremiah 9:1; Luke 7:11-15). It's amazing to think that in that same bottle and on those pages are the tears of my own father and mother when they said farewell to their dying parents and family members. Also stored in that container are my wife's tears she shed during the painful delivery of our children. And there, too, are the precious tears that fell from the tender cheeks of my kids when they realized they needed a Savior. God cares for us so much that He has not forgotten one salty drop that has ever fallen—or will ever fall—from our eyes. All our deepest groanings are kept in His care.

If you have a water bottle or a Bible with you in your pack, take them out and look at them, drink from both and remember God's great love for you!

O merciful and loving Father, thank You for the care You have given to my tears. I am humbled to know You have held on to them all this time. You alone are able to comfort me and cause me to forget the pain they represent. Blessed be Your name for this display of how much You love me. In Jesus, Your holy Son's name. Amen.

40

The Condo

Beware that you do not forget the LORD your God.
DEUTERONOMY 8:11

I sat beside my son, Nathan, in a treestand we affectionately called "The Condo." It bore that name because there was plenty of room in it for both of us. Our friend had built it with good sturdy lumber, and it featured a bench with a comfortable backrest. There was only one flaw. Due to the way one of the tree's limbs had grown, there was an open spot in the floor. To bypass the problem all we had to do when we climbed in was step around it. One of us had to straddle it with his feet when we were sitting. Nathan ended up at that spot.

The morning was quiet as we monitored the large field. There was no talking, just watching. After about 30 minutes I slowly turned my head to look at my son. His eyes were drooping and his head was beginning to bob. I could tell that the drool of dozing was only seconds away. When his shoulders slumped he leaned forward a little. Suddenly, out of nowhere, he let out a scream that seemed to shake the entire farm. After a moment's recovery he started to laugh. I controlled my disappointment that our hunt was probably over and asked him what had happened.

"Oh, Dad!" he stated with a noticeable shortness of breath. "I fell into a deep sleep. When I woke up and opened my eyes I was looking down. All I saw was the ground through the opening in the floor. I just knew I was falling out of the sky!" Thus the blood-curdling scream. Then we both had a good laugh that continues to this day each time we remember the incident.

Some hunters who have tumbled out of tree-stands after falling asleep in them might agree that too much comfort up there can be dangerous. The Condo is proof. It might have been better if there were some strategically placed nails in the seat or in the backrest to lightly dig at our flesh and keep us alert. Instead, it was cozy to a fault.

The hazard that excessive ease creates is not limited to treestands. For those of us who belong to God and who live in a nation that is blessed with so much wealth at our fingertips, a very real pitfall awaits. Allowing ourselves to become overly comfortable and knowingly relaxed in our abundant possessions is a dangerous state of heart. It can lead us to the tragedy of pridefully forgetting our need for God. The wandering Israelites in Moses' day proved this to be true over and over again. They watched God richly supply their every need, then they turned away from Him when their bellies were full. It's a sad commentary on one of the greatest weaknesses of mankind.

I could have spared Nathan his treestand trauma if I had elbowed him when I saw him beginning to drift into sleep. That would have salvaged the hunt. As for our potential to be too much at ease with our lives and disregard our dependency on our heavenly Father, the Holy Spirit wants us to heed His nudges now. He wants to deliver us in advance from the results of our complacency and help us be on the alert at all times. Take note of Moses' words of warning in Deuteronomy 8:11-14:

> Beware that you do not forget the LORD your God by not keeping His commandments…Otherwise, when you have eaten and are satisfied, and have built good houses…and your silver and gold multiply, and all that you have multiplies, then your heart will become proud and you will forget the LORD your God who brought you out from the land of Egypt, out of the house of slavery.

To not respond to this divine elbow in our fleshly sides will result in a very real fall! Take the time

today to remember who alone has abundantly supplied your needs.

*Father, thank You for Your bountiful provision.
I confess that all I have, will have, or ever hope
to have is from Your mighty and loving hands.
Help me never forget You in times of abundance
and remember to thank You for the gift of need.
It reminds me that I am hopeless without You.
Help my deepest longing to be for You and not
what You give. Blessed be Your name. Amen.*

41

Middle Seat

*He saw a large crowd,
and felt compassion for them.*

MATTHEW 14:14

Rarely had I longed for the solitude of a deerstand as much as the day Annie and I boarded a flight to Dallas. The overbooked plane exiled us to middle seats in separate rows surrounded by strangers. As I sat there, squeezed by my extra-large male neighbors, it wasn't long before I realized the fellow next to the window had some type of serious respiratory condition. His cough was preceded by a deep draw of air that was accompanied by a distinct and disturbing wheeze. The instant his lungs were at full capacity, he would begin his cough. It was one loud and continuous gurgling sound followed by several short, thrashing finishes. I was sure something had broken loose in his body the first time I heard it.

I cringed and tried to roll up into an impenetrable ball, hoping to repel any of the deadly germs that might escape the man's innards. It was a sickening experience. Fearing that he may have been a victim of some terminal form of cancer or other disease, I didn't say anything. I didn't want to risk offending him.

As if he weren't enough to deal with, an irritating problem started behind me. The amazing little girl was about five years old. She was using her seat-back tray to do her daily quota of handstands, and I was taking a beating. I kept waiting for her parents to correct her behavior, but they didn't. Along with the tiny pest behind me, across the aisle and two rows up were a couple of people who were talking loudly enough to compete with the volume of the jet engines. It might have been fine if their conversation had been interesting. Unfortunately, their loud prattle was boring and, at times, very lewd.

Needless to say, I was not a happy flyer. I knew the next two hours were going to be comparable to a root canal. I began to detest the bodies around me as well as everyone else on board. Though we were all divided by aisles and armrests, the crowd seemed to be closing in on me. I had no place to run.

Then, without warning, right in the middle of another lung-whipping cough next to me, a question came to my mind that made me uncomfortable: "If Jesus were sitting in this seat, how would He handle this situation?"

I felt embarrassed. My less-than-friendly feelings about those around me were generated by my complete lack of care for them. I didn't like the cougher, the kid, or the conversationalists. I had no affection for them, only rejection. I knew that Jesus' reaction, on the other hand, would have been quite different: "He saw a large crowd, and felt compassion for them."

The Savior would have likely healed the man sitting next to me, invited the child to come up and sit on His lap, and reasoned some sense into the talkers nearby. For Him, the flight would have been much too short, lacking the time to touch each one where he or she sat.

I was moved that day as I pondered my pitiful attitude in light of the Lord's love for people. I determined to do something about it. Before the plane landed in Dallas, I had managed to make a new friend. It was not the coughing machine next to me; he had finally gone to sleep (not dead, just asleep!). Instead, I discovered the other fellow was a delightful, young, first-time flyer who needed the comforting confidence of a veteran air traveler.

As I later reflected on my change of heart, I realized that while I was giving of myself to my row partner, I couldn't hear the sounds that had irritated me earlier. It's a phenomenon that seems to always occur when I look away from myself and see the needs of my neighbors. Being moved by compassion is as much a blessing to the one who extends it as it is to the one who receives it. Such is the way of Christ. Having His attitude of benevolence makes a long journey sweeter.

Thank You, Lord, for Your abundant compassion that You have shown me. You are worthy of my praise because You alone are good. Help me to see other people's needs as more important than my own. I know if I do, it will redeem the time You give to me here on earth. In Your kind and holy name I pray. Amen.

42

Guilty 'Til Proven Innocent

When you were dead in your transgressions…
He made you alive together with Him…
having canceled out the certificate of debt
consisting of decrees against us, which was
hostile to us; and He has taken it out of
the way, having nailed it to the cross.

COLOSSIANS 2:13,14

There is a rule of law in our land that is humanly fair and equitable for all who have allegedly committed crimes. Though they may be guilty of the deed, the law demands that they are "innocent until proven guilty." While this may be the rule in the courts, it is not one I carry into the woods when I go deer hunting.

Years ago, when I first began to pursue the wary whitetail, I learned very quickly that a sound I thought was merely the dainty scampering of a chipmunk or a squirrel was really a deer moving through the brush. Too many times I made the erroneous assumption that the sound was one critter's noise, when in fact it was that of another. After several misreads, I finally decided to consider every sound as suspect. I adopted that attitude and maintain it to this day. When I hear the slightest crunch in the leaves and can't identify the source by sight, I immediately think "guilty 'til proven innocent!" This method has yielded good results, and I have plenty of empty rifle shells and bloody, broken arrows to prove it.

There was a time in my life when, like an elusive buck trying to sneak past a hunter, I attempted to slip by God. It was my intent to get around His all-seeing eye and, without accountability to Him, enjoy the unholy pleasures of this world. I had no affection for God's ways, only contempt for His truth. In my heart of flesh there was nothing good. Like David confessed in Psalm 51:5: "Behold, I was brought forth in iniquity, and in sin my mother conceived me." My very thoughts were opposed to God's holiness. I was "by nature a child of wrath" (see Ephesians 2:3). Because I was born with a propensity to sin, I was doomed to be the target of the flaming arrows of God's judgment.

Thankfully, however, the Father of all things heard me and saw me and knew I was "guilty 'til proven innocent." I was *guilty* of having a sinful nature and needed desperately to be *made innocent*.

And, in the way that a passing whitetail could never make something different of itself, God knew I could in no way exonerate myself. It was then that the miracle of miracles happened! Colossians 1:21-22 describes it: "And although you were formerly alienated and hostile in mind, engaged in evil deeds, yet He has now reconciled you in His fleshly body through death, in order to present you before Him holy and blameless and beyond reproach." Thanks be to God that He saved me from the eternal consequences of my sinful nature! By accepting Christ I was transformed from impending death to eternal life. How great is His grace!

If you have allowed God to make you acceptable in His sight through Christ, rejoice! And, if you hear a sound that suddenly arouses your hunter's suspicion, let it remind you that God once heard you and found you.

Heavenly Father, thank You for canceling the certificate of debt that would have found me guilty. By nailing it to the cross of Your Son, Jesus, I have been made acceptable in Your

sight. Without that kind of love for me, I would surely have been sentenced to eternal destruction. Blessed be Your name and the name of Jesus, the blameless one, forever and ever. Amen.

43

Scoot Over

So show your love for the alien.

DEUTERONOMY 10:19

There is a farm I hunt near my home in Tennessee. It's a 15-mile drive on a rural highway lined with fields of tobacco crops. When spring arrives, they fill up with migrant workers, mostly from Mexico. The hundreds of individuals can be seen laboring tirelessly from planting time in May until harvest is completed near November. The population of the foreigners grows in number each year.

Many of the farmers who hire them and oversee their coming are very positive about their presence. One man told me he could not be happier with the work ethic he found in his laborers. Their willingness to work overshadowed their inability to communicate efficiently in English. He paid them a very good wage and said he looks forward to the new growing season so he can see the friends he has made over the past few years.

While the migrant laborers may be welcomed

by some, others have developed a contempt for the "different" workers. Some interesting conversations and quips can be heard at our local establishments. My ears have been privy to some less-than-kind remarks about those who bear little resemblance to the rest of us.

Each time I hear a derogatory statement about the foreigners in our land, I can't help but think of the command given to the Israelites through Moses in Deuteronomy 10:18-19: "He executes justice for the orphan and the widow, and shows His love for the alien by giving him food and clothing. So show your love for the alien, for you were aliens in the land of Egypt." The "outsiders" were tenderly linked with the orphan and the widow. This indicates the affection God must have for those who are displaced.

There is a truth that is overlooked by far too many people in our country. The immigrants that are visible to us, though temporary, are ultimately a gauge for the quality of our faith in Christ. If we treat them unkindly we are ignoring our former status as spiritual aliens. Consider these selected portions of Scripture:

> Remember that formerly you, the Gentiles in the flesh...were at that time separate from Christ, excluded from the commonwealth of Israel, and

strangers to the covenants of promise, having no hope and without God in the world. But now in Christ Jesus you who formerly were far off have been brought near by the blood of Christ. For He Himself is our peace, who made both groups into one and broke down the barrier of the dividing wall, by abolishing in His flesh the enmity (Ephesians 2:11-15).

Through Him we both have our access in one Spirit to the Father. So then you are no longer strangers and aliens, but you are fellow citizens with the saints, and are of God's household (verses 18,19).

What causes us to go from remembering to forgetting our former rank as aliens to Christ? And why would we mistreat the strangers among us? Perhaps it is the excessive comfort we have come to know and are not so willing to share. Or it may be a fear that "they" will become a permanent fixture in our landscape. For whatever reason, we withhold our kindness to foreigners, and this is a wrong and dangerous attitude. By not showing love for the alien we run the risk of gaining the displeasure of the One who has clothed and fed us by His love. The effects of His wrath are far greater than the small effort it takes to "scoot over" and let the newcomers have some room.

Since you are a hunter and your passion for the great outdoors takes you into the rural regions of America, you too may be seeing more foreigners these days. Or maybe a growing number of aliens have moved in to your town. Wherever you are, if your good attitude toward foreign workers is being challenged, use it to help you never forget that at one time God was kind to you when you were lost, and He welcomed you into His family.

O God, thank You for the love You have shown to every person through Your Son. Help me never forget how You made me a part of Your household even though I was a stranger. I pray for grace to extend Your love to others who have come to this country. Forgive me for the times I have failed in this regard. In Jesus' name. Amen.

44

Seize the Moment

Sanctify Christ as Lord in your hearts,
always being ready to make a defense to everyone
who asks you to give an account for the hope
that is in you, yet with gentleness and reverence.

1 PETER 3:15

I have seen and heard some interesting ways that folks have made known the sobering truth that someday all of us will meet our Maker. One of my favorite examples took place in Knoxville, Tennessee. A farmer owned some land at one end of a regional commercial airport. Though personally I never saw it, I was told that on a hillside, for all passengers and crew to see as they departed the runway, the farmer had constructed a message. I'm not sure what material he used, but the words were, "PREPARE TO MEET THY GOD!"

I have a feeling the cleverly placed warning found its way into many a heart, especially if there was turbulence on takeoff or a sudden, unusual mechanical noise. The nervous souls were probably quite moved by the truth in the farmer's message. I'm not sure if the guy's sermon on his mount is still there, but I have no doubt that it remains in the minds and hearts of those who saw it.

Another timely delivery of the "get ready" message was made by my son, Nathan. He was 15 years old when he and I were walking down our sidewalk on the way to our van. Annie and our daughter, Heidi, were already aboard, along with some precious friends who were visiting. It was Sunday morning, and we were going to church. For some strange reason I asked, "Son, would you like to drive us?" His learner's permit was a just a few weeks old, and I honestly don't know what possessed me to put our guests in such danger.

Before I could recant, Nathan excitedly responded, "Oh, Dad, I'd love to!"

I gave him the keys and he climbed into the driver's seat. I got in through the side door, smiled at our company, sat down in my seat, and put on my helmet. (Okay, the helmet part is not true.) Nathan started the engine and, as I had taught him, let it warm up before driving away. During the brief wait he decided to do a little evangelism. He turned in his chair and looked back through the van. Everyone knew he was a novice driver, and there was a certain tension in the air. With a sheepish grin, he asked, "Is everyone..." He paused just long enough for all of his passengers to look his way, then finished the question with a loud, "...saved?"

I'm sure his well-timed inquiry was as much for me as anyone else. He knew how unsettled I was by allowing him to drive, so he seized the moment. That boy is sharp! We all got a good laugh, then secretly tightened our safety belts when Nathan turned to face the front. (Obviously, we survived the day.)

Taking advantage of opportunity is a key to effective evangelism. As we go about our daily lives, whether on the job, in a crowd, or in the woods with friends, let's make the moments count by spreading the word about our eventual meeting with God. The fact is undeniable: "It is appointed for men to die once and after this comes judgment" (Hebrews 9:27). What hope can we offer to those who hear our message and are filled with terror? John 3:16: "For God so loved the world, that He gave His only begotten Son, that whoever believes in Him shall not perish, but have eternal life."

Someone offered this sobering advice: "Tell them that Jesus died for them. It will cost you nothing to say it, but it will cost them everything not to know!" How true.

Father in heaven, thank You for Your provision of salvation through Your blessed Son, Jesus. Thank You that someone took the time to tell me that You alone can save. Help me recognize opportunities to share this good news with others and have the boldness to seize the moment. Until You come I pray in Jesus' name. Amen.

45

Leaves of Three, Let It Be

Go your way, from now on sin no more.
JOHN 8:11

I'm among the unfortunate many who have skin that reacts unfavorably (to put it mildly) to the menacing botanical creeper commonly called poison ivy. Being a bow hunter who likes to enter the woods as early as August to check on and move deer stands, I'm often hiking along paths inhabited by the green monster. And when I see the dreaded beast, I can't help but remember the worst case of rash I've ever heard of.

My cousin was about 13 when he went with several of his friends on a day hike. They weren't quite as prepared as they should have been in terms of what they needed to pack for the adventure. One of the necessities they forgot was toilet paper. Facing a desperate need for that amenity, my cousin reached for the closest alternative. Unable to identify his choice of flora and unaware of the ancient rule that says

"Leaves of three, let it be," he made a terrible mistake. (I'm sure you're already wincing at the thought!)

All was well for the rest of the day, and they returned home exhausted but happy. Around midnight my cousin realized something didn't feel right. By mid-morning he was in a really bad way and realized he had an emergency on his hands (literally), as well as in another place that is very delicate. He was rushed to the emergency room and endured nearly a week of treatment in the hospital. With britches full of residual pain that lasted much longer than he cared to admit, the intense itching finally subsided but left "behind" scars of a lesson learned the hard way.

In contemplating this green menace to society, I've asked, as you probably have, "Is there anything redeemable about poison ivy?" The answer? "Of course!" Though the growth is an annoying and dangerous threat to the skin, there are at least two spiritually valuable insights to be gained.

The first is that to avoid the plant we have to know how to recognize it. And when it comes to our souls, learning to recognize sin when we see it is paramount to steering clear of it. Job prayed, "How many are my iniquities and sins? Make known to me my rebellion and my sins" (Job 13:23). Job knew the painful progression of sin that is so similar to what happens with poison ivy. Sin often doesn't hurt at first, but later on the effects can be excruciating. James warns, "Each [person] is tempted when he is carried away and enticed by his own lust. Then when lust has conceived, it gives birth to sin; and when sin is accomplished, it brings forth death" (James 1:14-15).

If we know what tends to entice us, we can watch for it and make sure we "lay aside...the sin which so easily entangles us" (Hebrews 12:1). That lets us continue on our life journey through the woods of life in a safe and enjoyable way.

The second "benefit" to poison ivy is that it forces us to learn what to do when our bodies come into contact with this dreaded plant. In our spiritual lives, most of us have to admit that from time to time we allow the poisonous oil of willful sin to permeate our hearts. That being true, knowing the best remedy and how to apply it when it happens is an absolute must. Thankfully, there's a prescription available at the "divine pharmacy": "If we confess our sins, He is faithful and righteous to forgive us our sins and to cleanse us from all unrighteousness" (1 John 1:9).

Oh what wonderful medicine that passage is for any of us who are, perhaps at this very moment, dealing with the agonizing results of britches full of itches.

Apply the healing balm now! And as the relief and healing take place, determine to live from now on by the clear instructions for avoiding disaster found in Jesus' words: "Go. From now on sin no more" (John 8:11). You'll be glad—I promise! And your hike through life's wilderness won't go through verdant green valleys that cause rashes of unrighteousness.

Lord, please have mercy on me. Forgive me for letting the poisonous touch of iniquity scar my life. Wash my wounds and provide Your healing balm of forgiveness and mercy. Help me recognize and avoid the danger of the ungodliness that lurks in this world. In Jesus' name I pray. Amen.

46

Next Time

Go lie down, and it shall be if He calls you,
that you shall say, "Speak LORD…"

1 SAMUEL 3:9

A young boy went to live with his grandfather on
a farm in one of the Carolinas. The granddad
had been an avid deer hunter most of his life, but
the motivation to get up predawn and go to a stand
waned as he headed into his mid-sixties. Perhaps
it was being a widower and having a pared-down
need for filling a freezer or maybe it was simply his
reluctance to risk a back injury by attempting an
unaided drag of a heavy carcass out of the woods.
For whatever reason, he simply didn't go as often.
But with the arrival of a youngster who had an itch
for hunting that needed to be scratched, the grandfather felt a renewed excitement for the idea of the
pursuit. For the first time in a few years, he could
barely wait for autumn to come and bring with it the
fall hunting season.

The grandfather looked forward to seeing his

grandson's youthful eyes light up when he got his first sighting of a deer from the viewpoint of a deer stand. He knew it would be especially thrilling to coach the boy in the art of learning to read the subtle signs of a deer's presence. Helping him look closely through the foliage to recognize the shape of a deer's motionless body or the unique color of its fur would be sheer pleasure. And assisting him in seeing the hard-to-notice visual evidences of a deer, such as the flicker of an ear or a tail, would be pure fun.

Finally the first day of gun season arrived. Well before daylight the two of them were huddled together in a buddy-type ladder stand that leaned against a tree about 30 yards inside the woods. The stand was very well placed and in sight of a healthy food plot. The granddad knew the female deer would likely be the early evening visitors to the field. Around 4:30 in the afternoon the boy was instructed, "Josh, it's just about now that the does are getting up and starting to move toward this field. They get hungry just like you and me, and some of them will come here for supper. I want you to start looking right now, keeping your eyes keyed in on the area and your ears wide open for unusual sounds."

About 15 minutes later the grandson whispered, "Grandpa, do you hear that?"

Granddad quietly responded, "I don't hear anything. Keep listening." Less than a minute later the boy repeated, "Did you hear that, Grandpa?"

"No...keep listening."

Another two or three minutes went by.

"Gramps, you heard that, didn't you?"

"Son, I ain't hearin' nuthin'...now just keep your ears open."

Suddenly it dawned on the old fellow what was happening. He realized it had been a long time since he'd been in the woods, and he was overlooking the fact that his hearing wasn't what it used to be. Realizing that his grandson had likely been hearing the barely audible and light pressing of dried leaves being made by deer hooves, he whispered, "Josh, next time you hear that sound you've been hearing, I want you to tell me what direction you think it's coming from and how far away you think it is."

Not more than 30 seconds later the grandson slowly shoved his elbow into his Granddad's side and very quietly said, "It's coming from behind us, Gramps, and it sounds really close!"

"Josh, I want you to very slowly put your thumb on the hammer of your gun and get ready. I'm thinking there's a deer right behind us that's going to move under us on its way to the field. If we're right about this, let the deer get out in front of us before you raise your gun."

The report of the rifle and the sight of the doe going down at the field's edge was followed by some rambunctious, congratulatory back whacking. As Josh celebrated bagging his first deer, his Grandpa basked in the warm glow of the fires of excitement... something he hadn't felt in many years.

This story reminds me of what happened to young Samuel and the much older priest Eli. This event is recorded in the Bible in 1 Samuel 3. Not knowing the Lord's voice and never having had God talk directly to him, Samuel thought it was Eli who was calling him in the night. He went to Eli three times saying, "Here I am!" That's when it dawned on the aging and experienced Eli that Samuel was hearing from God. The priest told the young boy, "Go lie down, and it shall be if He calls you [again], that you shall say, "Speak, LORD, for Your servant is listening." It did happen again, and Samuel responded just as Eli instructed. As a result of Eli's guidance, Samuel learned to recognize the voice of God. Eventually the boy became a celebrated prophet.

What satisfaction Eli must have felt to help Samuel recognize and respond to God's voice that night. And I'm sure Josh's grandfather can relate to

Eli's joy. May the Lord give many more of us opportunities to know the delight of assisting others with their hunts...for deer and for salvation.

Lord, thank You for those times when I'm privileged to see the light of excitement in the eyes of younger hunters and seekers of Your truth. May I seize every opportunity to teach them how to hear Your voice. In Jesus' name I pray. Amen.

47

Not Just Walking

Let us go up to the mountain of the LORD...
that He may teach us concerning His ways
and that we may walk in His paths.

ISAIAH 2:3

I know I need to exercise in the off-season to stay in good shape for hunting. Exercise is a definite requirement for being prepared for the energy-consuming rigors of chasing deer up and down Tennessee hills during open seasons. My choice of keeping my muscles and cardiovascular condition in good order is to walk briskly. I used to thoroughly enjoy the aerobic and muscular benefits of long-distance runs, but my running career came to a bitter end.

In my younger days I started training as a runner with a goal to complete a full-length marathon. After several 5k, 10k, half-marathon, and uncounted training runs, I finally felt ready for "the long one." In December one year, right after Christmas, I completed an official 26.2 mile run in South Carolina! I was graced with a nice medal, a T-shirt, and one other thing my wife warned me might happen: knee surgery.

Thanks to the wise guidance of the folks in the physical therapy/rehabilitation department at our post-operation facility, I recovered nicely. However, the over-the-road, joint-pounding, 7- to 8-minute mile runs had to be eliminated and replaced with low-impact, cartilage-friendly walking. So at least four times a week during non-hunting months, I lace up my tennis shoes, put on my sweats, and trek a 12- to 14-minute mile (hopefully). For the past several years I've been able to do this without rewounding my knee.

If you had approached me in the middle of my years as a "serious runner" and said, "Someday you'll love just walking," I would've looked at you like you had stinky sneakers coming out your ears. But today I can say you were right! I happily admit that I'm glad I put on the walking miles…and for more reasons than the health benefits.

Exercise, whether its running or walking, requires sacrifice. At least it does for me. Its something I know I *must* do in order to take care of my "ticker" and to keep the pounds down. But to do it, I must give up valuable time, energy, and fun. And the same is true regarding other essential things I have to do. Praying requires discipline. Writing lyrics takes concerted mental effort and controlled thoughts. Thinking through business matters demands focus. Keeping up my singing/vocal chops and guitar playing means working at details and form. Since I'm using the discipline needed to get out there and walk, I add these other must-dos to make the time go more quickly and to accomplish more! My walking routine for exercise enables my ability to practice the disciplines of spiritual growth.

The apostle Paul said, "Everyone who competes in the games exercises self-control in all things. They then do it to receive a perishable wreath, but we an imperishable. Therefore I run in such a way, as not without aim…I discipline my body and make it my slave" (1 Corinthians 9:25-27).

I'm grateful for deer season because it motivates me to willfully exercise all year long so I can be tireless as I stalk game on our steep hills. But I'm also grateful for how the discipline of walking has reached into the other more important areas of my daily life and given me benefits beyond measure.

Lord, please continue to teach me Your ways as I walk with You. Grant me the strength to be self-controlled in all areas of my life so I can experience the everlasting wreath of Your favor. In Jesus' name. Amen.

48

The Shell

*The Lord gave and the
Lord has taken away.*

JOB 1:21

On the way to an evening deerstand location I
stopped and randomly picked up a handful
of acorns and put them in my pocket. After settling
into my stand I dug them out and began crack-
ing the shells open, removing the nut, and partially
squashing them. My plan was to drop them around
my stand, letting the odor of the fresh meat of the
acorn serve as an attractant. Then I came upon a
particular nut that looked totally normal...except it
was noticeably lighter in weight.

Curious about the reason for its weightlessness,
I turned the shell around in my fingers and discovered a tiny hole. I cracked the nut. A worm or some
other boring insect had drilled its way in, consumed
the innards, and then left. That little bug probably
thought it was leaving behind nothing but a worthless acorn shell. What it didn't know was that it left

behind much more than an empty container. To me it was an incredibly profound picture of the life of a man in the Old Testament. His name was Job.

As one of the best-known examples of someone who undeservedly suffered loss, Job went from being wealthy and healthy one day to being in distress and poverty the next. Death and destruction took his children and possessions. Then he developed sores all over his body. Adding to his despair, his wife, rather than comforting him with tender care, encouraged him to end his misery by cursing God. Job's friends were no help either. They gathered to console him… but ended up condemning him instead. Everyone thought God had abandoned this man…so he must not be as righteous as he appeared. Yet as terrible as his dilemma was, Job's life ended positively.

Job's journey from being filled to being emptied returned to being filled. God generously returned Job's prosperity and provided a new family. Job 42:10 and 12 reports, "The LORD restored the fortunes of Job when he prayed for his friends, and the LORD increased all that Job had twofold…The LORD blessed the latter days of Job more than his beginning." But of all the material things that were given back to Job, there was something unseen that was of greater value. The confidence that God is faithful and worthy to be totally trusted had to be the most precious by far.

While Job's suffering is of a caliber almost inconceivable by most of us, there are some who can identify with his distress. Affliction, tragedy, adversity, and loss of every sort has befallen some of us. And fully understanding the purpose of such events is nearly impossible. Yet how many times have we heard someone testify after suffering greatly, "I wouldn't take anything for what I've been through." And when asked how they could possibly say such a thing, many respond, "In the midst of this experience I gained the greatest awareness of God's grace, presence, power, and peace. I gained the assurance that God is truly God."

The empty acorn shell I held that morning on the deerstand went into my pocket. I took it home as a reminder of Job's life. When suffering comes and loss is experienced, there are divine purposes that will one day be revealed...and redeemed...in miraculous ways that only God can accomplish.

Shell of a Man

There was no good reason that I could see
Why anything that was everything was taken from me

My heart felt like a tomb that was waiting for the dead
That's when I went to the Savior and said,

"I'm just a shell of a man, Lord
And You know I wish I could bring You more."
But then He said, "Son, you're the one I'm looking for
'Cause if I'm gonna give you everything I am
What I need is just a shell of a man."

Giving up so much wasn't easy to do
But it had to be done so He could make room
For the mountain of joy and a river of peace
I'll never forget when I fell on my knees and said,

"I'm just a shell of a man, Lord
And You know I wish I could bring You more."
But then He said, "Son, you're the one I'm looking for
'Cause if I'm gonna give you everything I am
What I need is just a shell of a man."

*God, when I'm emptied of all, please fill me with
You 100 percent. In Jesus' name I pray. Amen.*

49

Still Yielding

They will still yield fruit in old age.

PSALM 92:14

In the southeast region of the country where I live, hunting deer from treestands is very common, especially for bow hunters. We have a lot of tall, straight tree choices to attach a climber to, and the telephone-pole tree trunks are great for climbing sticks and lock-on platform combinations. We also have plenty of timber types that are excellent for leaning a ladder stand on and cinching it down safely with ratchet straps.

Why do so many around here opt for treestands? Being suspended above a deer's keen sight field and being high enough that our natural human odors, such as breath and...well...other aromas, can drift above their super-sensitive nostrils definitely give hunters an advantage. For that reason, I've been in every tree in the woods in Tennessee. (Well, okay, I know that I've at least hugged more than my share!)

One thought that comes to my mind while sitting

high in a tree on my portable metal platform is the same thought I suspect many other hunters have: *What if this tree suddenly decides to give up the ghost and fall down?* When that horrid image disturbs my tranquility, I quickly dismiss it and fight the momentary shivers of fear. This fear isn't pure conjecture though. It's based on fact. In my time in the woods, I've seen quite a few trees fall for seemingly no reason.

While sitting in my climber on a hunt in a nearby county, there was suddenly an odd sound about 40 yards straight in front of me. All at once a rather young-looking tree toppled over. There was no heavy wind (I wouldn't have been in a tree if there was) and the woods were nearly dead silent. It was very eerie. The tree seemed to simply succumb to…well, to what I don't know…and crashed to the ground. The memory of that sight haunts me from time to time as I'm sitting quietly among tree branches waiting for deer to move in close.

The remedy for the risk involved in hunting by hanging out in trees is to check the trunk closely for disease before deciding to use it. While this isn't a guarantee, feeling as confident as possible about a tree's health gives me comfort. I've made this check for rot a self-imposed policy. Also, in most cases, my preferred choice is an older tree that is heavier, wider, and stronger.

The reason I favor trees with significant age is the likelihood that their roots run deep. Some signs that nature has seen to it that a "senior citizen" of the woods is planted well is if there's sap and the leaves are very green. If the tree is nut bearing, finding fruit among its branches or on the ground below is further evidence that it is strong and safe. If I find one of these trees in a good location in terms of deer movement, that's where I'll hang a stand and feel quite at ease spending time on it.

There's a beautiful connection that can be made between reliable old trees and trustworthy older men and women. Older folks have qualities that allow them to handle the extra weight they're asked to bear:

> Planted in the house of the LORD, they will flourish in the courts of our God. They will still yield fruit in old age; they shall be full of sap and very green (Psalm 92:13-14).

For the aged tree, the extra load it must bear is very important. That load is me...nearly 200 pounds of hunter. For the "tree of flesh" that I am, the added weight of responsibility put on me is far more valuable:

To declare that the LORD is upright; He is my rock, and there is no unrighteousness in Him (verse 15).

The critical question for this "aging oak" is, *Am I firmly planted in the house of the Lord so that I can be trusted with testifying to God's righteousness?* My sincere desire—and probably yours too—is that this is true!

Father, thank You for the good soil of Your presence so I can grow old and yet be strong and bear Your fruit in my old age. Help me to never allow unrighteousness to uproot my life in You. To Your glory I pray. Amen.

50

That Boy of Mine

This is My beloved Son,
in whom I am well-pleased.

MATTHEW 3:17

The wild game dinner was well-attended. As the main speaker, I was glad to see a lot of fathers and their teen sons at the tables. After the event, when the crowd was dispersing, I shook the hands of several attendees as they filed out of the huge room. I'll never forget one quick exchange I had with one of the dads. He was with his son, who looked to be 12 or 13. The dad had his arm around the boy's neck and spoke with a huge smile and a southern drawl.

"This boy right here is the best hunter in the state. He knows how to find 'em, set-up on 'em, and he does as good a job trackin' 'em after the shot as anybody I hunt with. And I've never seen a young feller so mindful of safety as this boy. Ain't nobody else I'd rather hunt with than my son."

I could tell the dad's words were coming from a grateful heart. Though it was quite clear he was proud of how good the youngster was in the woods, it seemed that he was more thankful that his best hunting buddy was his son. But the dad's expression of joy wasn't the only thing that caught my attention.

As the father delivered his words of pride in his son's hunting prowess, I glanced at the young man. He was grinning so big I thought his ears would pop off. Though the boy didn't say a word during our momentary visit, I could tell his heart was screaming with delight at his father's praise.

I didn't get a chance to say it to the dad, but the kind words he spoke about his son had a nice biblical ring. As recorded in Matthew 3:17, God offered some profound praise when Jesus was baptized. The people in the area heard a voice from heaven say, "This is My beloved Son, in whom I am well-pleased." One similarity between what the dad said after the wild game dinner and what God said at the Jordan River is that the words were said *about* the sons, not *to* them. Though the Bible doesn't state it, can't you just picture God's joy and Jesus' pleasure at such a powerful confirmation of Father/Son love and respect? I can't help but imagine a big grin and the glow of acceptance on Jesus' face when the unseen voice boomed from heaven.

If you have a hard time telling your sons and

daughters that you love them, one way to let them know you care is to say complimentary words *about* them to others, making sure your kids are in earshot. This will thrill them down deep and help build up your ability to share with them face-to-face your heartfelt words of love. Let your children know often how much you care and how proud you are of them. You'll see them smile, build their self-confidence, and strengthen your relationship. It's a win–win all the way around!

That Boy of Mine

I turned the corner down on Tenth and Main
And some grandma's broken-down old car was in my
    lane
Some young kid was under the hood
    trying to make it run
And when I drove by I realized…well, that's my son!

That boy of mine sure does make me proud
I want to tell everybody and say it loud
I could search the whole world over and never find
Another one like him—that boy of mine

It scared me to my knees on the day he came
I prayed, "God help me raise him right, in Jesus' name"

And in spite of me he turned out as good as they come
And that grandma's car is in good hands—
    he'll get it done

There's not a thing he needs to do to win my love
He belongs to me, and to me, that's good enough

But that boy of mine sure does make me proud
I want to tell everybody and say it loud
I could search the whole world over and never find
Another one like him—that boy of mine

Father in heaven, thank You for speaking such memorable words to Your Son at the Jordan River. Give those of us who are "parents not in heaven" the courage to follow Your example and bless our children with kind, loving, and affirming words. Give me an opportunity today to tell my kids I love them. In Your Son's name I pray. Amen.

51

The Bones Testify

*[Joseph said,] You shall carry
my bones up from here.*

GENESIS 50:25

Though it isn't uncommon to find the bones of
deceased deer in the woods, for me there is something strangely emotional about it. Very often my
imagination runs a little wild as I wonder...

- How did it die?
- Did it suffer?
- Was it mortally wounded by an arrow, a
  bullet, a car, or a predator?
- What was its life like?

The answers to the questions are impossible to
know without major forensic investigation, but one
thing the discovery of a skeleton reveals is that the
animal was alive at one time. In truth, dead bones are
the lingering testimony of many other details about
the animal besides its existence, including a birth

took place, the newborn was cared for by its family, the coming of spring was enjoyed, hot summers were endured, God provided sustenance through the fruit of the land, cold winters were tolerated, and if they lived long enough, very likely the process of procreation was experienced. The bones also testify to the inevitable ending of life through death.

Its quite amazing to think that all that information can be in a single rib fragment, a piece of a hip bone, or a jaw section from a bleached skull. Bones, whether in part or whole, tell a story. Perhaps this truth is what Joseph knew when he made his brothers solemnly swear they would carry his bones out of Egypt. He did not want to be buried in a place where God had been replaced by idols and where he'd been a captive. He wanted to be buried in the land he believed God would provide for His people and where God would be freely worshiped.

For hundreds of years Joseph's bones were carried around and carefully cared for by the generations that followed him and his brothers. No doubt, each time the container of bones was handled there was a testimony given regarding his presence on the earth, the importance he placed in family, God's divine and faithful provision, and the brevity of life. All that encouragement was in a pile of old bones. Isn't that amazing?

The next time you come across the bleached and clean bony remains of a deer, why not take a few pieces home with you and create an artful display? And then each time you see it, you'll be reminded that someday, like the deer's bones tell a story, like Joseph's bones sent a message, your skeleton will testify to your existence. The question to ask now is, *What will my bones testify of?* Will it be a life dedicated to Christ? To family? To helping others? To contributing to the body of Christ?

O God who gives life, I pray that You will cause me to consider daily the testimony that my life and death will leave when people remember me. May it be one that brings You glory. In Your Son's name I pray. Amen.

52

The Comparison

Suddenly, they shoot at [the blameless].

PSALM 64:4

If your favorite way to hunt deer is with archery equipment, if you thrive on the thrill of making yourself nearly disappear in the woods, and if sharpening your arrows is one of your favorite forms of entertainment, then brace yourself. I have some news for both of us that might be hard to take. Archers are sometimes used to picture someone wicked. If this news has you all riled up right now—hey, I didn't originate the comparison. The connection comes right out of the Bible. You'll find it in more than one place, but I'll highlight one prominent place where the finger of bad association is pointed at us. Read it and weep.

> Hear my voice, O God, in my complaint; preserve my life from dread of the enemy. Hide me from the secret counsel of evildoers, from the tumult of those who do iniquity, who have sharpened their tongue like a sword. They aimed bitter speech

as their arrow, to shoot from concealment at the blameless; suddenly they shoot at him, and do not fear (Psalm 64:1-4).

Now don't shoot me, the messenger of this biblical description. Keep in mind that this passage is from a psalm *David* wrote. And he was a fellow lover of the outdoors. Remember David? Shepherding, hillside musings at the marvels of creation, slings, stones, Goliath killing? If anyone understood how his enemy might hunt him like an animal, David, the slayer of a lion and a bear, surely did. Even his words tell us he knows something about the unique nuances of a hunt: sharpened, aimed, arrow, concealment. These all are familiar to every archer, and I'm sure they twang your bow string.

So what can we do about this seemingly unfair comparison of our way of life to the wicked? I decided to mull this over. After a while I realized something: David wasn't comparing us to the wicked. No, he was comparing the wicked to the hunter. The similarity isn't a slam against us, it's a compliment to them!

David needed a clear, effective way to describe the cunningness of the evildoers. At the top of his list of those who can successfully pursue prey were the users of swords and arrows. In realizing this, suddenly I felt honored instead of dishonored. I don't believe

David wanted to offend those of us who bend the bow. Why? The answer is further down the text in verse 7. Read it and leap!

God will shoot at [the wicked] with an arrow; suddenly they will be wounded.

Now look who we're in the picture with. Does that make you feel better? I certainly do.

God, thank You for the invention of the bow and the arrow. Thank You for the way it can be used to provide sustenance. I appreciate the biblical fact that as an archer, You are one of us...and we are one with You through Your Son. Amen.

53

The Strike

He spreads His lightning about Him…
Its noise declares His presence.

JOB 36:30,33

The sky was pitch black when I got into my truck to make the 20-minute drive to my friend's farm for a morning hunt. The humidity level was high, but the winds were calm. As far as I could tell, the weather would be tolerable for a predawn entry to my stand. When I turned onto the nearby interstate and got up to cruising speed, I reached down to turn the radio on. That's when it happened.

K-bam!

I can't adequately put into words the intense, sudden fear that gripped me as my eyes saw only white and my hearing was reduced to a deafening hiss. I carefully but quickly lifted my foot to find the brake pedal as I whispered a prayer of thanks that at such an early hour I was alone on the two westbound lanes. I know I weaved back and forth as I tried to

get oriented, keep on the pavement, and slow down…
all at the same instant.

What happened? One of the most incredible
displays of God's creative power I've ever witnessed!
What I remember seeing was a brilliant, white bolt
of lightning about ten inches wide, round in shape,
with streaks of yellowish fire and serrated edges. The
details are pressed into my mind because as I was
reaching for the radio I was looking toward the side
of the road…at the exact place and time the lightning
ball engulfed the metal road sign I was passing. The
best I can tell, the strike took place a mere ten yards
from where I sat in my pickup.

Within seconds my vision returned. My hands
shook as I slowed to a crawl and found my lane again.
I continued down the road toward my exit, feeling
vulnerable and yet very excited. I realized just how
much at the mercy of God's grace we humans can be
in the face of nature's fireworks. I was elated that I'd
seen—and survived!—such an awesome sight.

I debated whether to continue to my stand that
morning. I decided to do what any serious and wise
deer hunter would do. I drove to the farm. When I
arrived and got out of the truck, I didn't hurry into
the woods. I stood a while, scrutinized the atmo-
sphere, and listened to the radio for a weather report.

I decided to wait until daylight started to appear so I could get a good view of the sky. After a short while, confident that the impending storm had passed, I trekked to my stand…with a certain tenseness and a total willingness to not linger for one moment if the sky turned darker. After all, I would be sitting in a *metal* stand holding a muzzle loader made of *metal*. It didn't take a rocket psychologist to understand the risk in that deadly combo.

As I pondered what had happened on the highway that morning, the two things that struck me were how amazingly quick the lightning had appeared and the unbelievably loud noise made when it hit.

At the time of the bolt blast, I didn't connect it with a passage in Job that highlights the sound. The passage is in chapter 36, verses 30 and 33: "He spreads His lightning about Him…Its noise declares His presence." When I read those lines I remembered that morning on the Interstate. I whispered, "So that's what the presence of God sounds like!" Wow! A reverent and humbly renewed determination to be at peace with such an awesome God immediately came over me.

Father, when You cover Your hands with lightning and command it to strike its mark, You reveal Your greatness. Help me to always respect Your majesty and notice and be in awe of the powerful earthly representatives of Your awesomeness. In Jesus' name I pray. Amen.

54

The Watcher

*Behold, the eye of the LORD is on
those who fear Him.*

PSALM 33:18

A soft, nearly inaudible crunch in the leaves was the only sound the mature buck produced as he slowly nosed the ground for a late September browse. His demeanor was relaxed, and it was obvious he believed he was alone in the woods. What he didn't know was the dread he wanted to avoid—me!—was just above him...only 16 feet away.

My decision to rise long before the first light of day, my careful and intentional almost silent entry into the predawn woods that morning, and my sufficient use of scent suppression had yielded at last the sweet fruit of opportunity. Directly below the portable aluminum platform on which I stood was the reward of all my efforts. For a brief few minutes I silently gloated in an accomplishment that happens only ever so often for a whitetail deer hunter.

What was taking place was glorious to enjoy.

Essentially I had traded roles with the whitetail. Usually he was the one who would be standing camouflaged among the shapes and colors of the foliage-laden woods, watching me as I attempted to slip into his home without being noticed. The number of times my trying-to-be-quiet presence had resulted in a deer's sudden, unexpected, heart-stopping, snort-blasting escape are far too numerous to count. However, on this day, I was the privileged one, blending in with the patterns on the wallpaper of his living room as he ambled in. I was totally invisible to him at that moment.

While I waited for the buck to present the broadside of his massive body, I closely studied his behavior. I knew what I'd learned from past encounters with deer was the very same knowledge that was assisting me this morning. Because I believe that "today's hunt can be tomorrow's guide," I kicked my intake of information into high gear.

As I stood above the deer and added arrows of know-how to my quiver of hunting experience, something suddenly caught the buck's attention. Perhaps it was a slight, unfelt downdraft that carried a hint of my breath to his nose or maybe it was a trace of scent I had errantly left behind on a low-hanging branch I'd brushed against on my way to my stand.

Whatever the cause, the buck went on full alert. He knew something or someone was there...but where? He put his nose into the air, raised his tail slowly, and then, with deliberate steps, he turned back in the direction from which he came. He didn't bolt and run. Instead he cautiously walked out of my reality and back into my dreams.

When the sun went down that day, as far as I know that old buck was still among the living. Though disappointed, I didn't leave the woods completely empty handed. As I often do, I will ponder the challenging moment until I see something morally or spiritually useful in it. It's my beneficial way of revenging the defeat.

That smart old buck beneath my stand seemed casual and relaxed until he suddenly sensed he wasn't alone. That's when his behavior completely changed. In the same way, there have been times in my life when I've allowed myself to be lulled into a dangerous feeling of aloneness—the kind that convinces me I can proceed with a questionable decision or choice without being seen. Then, in a merciful and timely way, the invisible wind of the Holy Spirit sends a message to my heart: "The ways of a man are before the eyes of the LORD, and He watches all his paths" (Proverbs 5:21). Ouch.

Like the buck I encountered that morning that didn't hesitate to respond to whatever it was that triggered his senses, in those moments of "pre-sin," I usually manage to catch the whiff of the biblical absolute that the Watcher has me in His view. My demeanor changes in a pronounced way. I become keenly aware of how I'm acting, what I'm contemplating, and where I'm going. Then I turn toward my God, determined to pursue righteousness.

The next time you've done enough right things as a hunter to make you "the watcher" in the deer's home, I encourage you to keep in mind that as you sit quietly with your eyes on a deer, don't forget you're not the only watcher in the woods.

He's Watching

Whatever you're doing behind that door
Don't forget, the eyes of the Lord are watching.
They can see you
You can pull those shades, pull them way down low
And think nobody sees who you really are, but He
    knows
'Cause He's watching. He can see you

Nothing is hidden, nothing gets by
Nothing is hidden, from the all-seeing eyes of the Lord
Oh…He can see you

You can wait until the sun goes down
And in the cover of the nighttime you can sneak around
But He's watching. He can see you

But if you lift those shades
And open that door
If you walk in the light
You won't have to worry anymore
That He's watching. Oh…He can see you

'Cause nothing is hidden, nothing gets by
Nothing is hidden from the all-seeing eyes of the Lord
Oh…He can see you

55

When the Wolf Comes Near

The wolf snatches them, and scatters them.

JOHN 10:12

If you're a parent and a deer hunter who lives and hunts in one of the Western states, or if you've ever hunted in that region, you might have seen or heard a wolf. I've never encountered one, but just the possibility sends chills up my Eastern spine.

In my mind the wolf is one of the most mysterious creatures that roam our planet. Its shadowlike aloofness, its legendary silhouette that can suddenly appear in the mist, its chilling stare, and its lonely and unnerving song in the night keeps my respect level high. I know that many folks—such as frontiersmen, explorers, hunters, and farmers—have encountered the cunning predator on mountainsides and in forests with uneventful outcomes, but many others haven't been as fortunate. That's why I'm satisfied to go through life only imagining what it would be like to meet up with one.

The fear that the sight or sound of a wolf can

instantly pour into the heart must have been what
was referred to when Jesus said,

> I am the good shepherd; the good shepherd lays
> down His life for the sheep. He who is a hired
> hand, and not a shepherd, who is not the owner
> of the sheep, sees the wolf coming and leaves the
> sheep, and flees, and the wolf snatches them and
> scatters them. He flees because he is a hireling, and
> is not concerned about the sheep (John 10:11-13).

The reason I include parents in the opening sentence of these thoughts about the wolf is because of a
sobering picture I saw in those words of Jesus. There
is an analogy that we would do well to see. Maybe the
following lyrical rendition of the passage will bring it
to your attention. Your little lambs—your children—
might benefit. They certainly deserve it!

When the Wolf Comes Near

The sheep are up on the hill tonight
And he sits near the fire
He's not the shepherd, he's just the one for hire
Then at the edge of the dancing firelight
They suddenly appear
Those eyes that glow with the taste of blood
And he knows
The wolf is near

Well he trembles as he whispers,
"These sheep are not my own
Why should I be concerned?"
And in an instant he was gone
While the sheep were scattered and stolen
He was flying down the hill
He had his life…
And the wolf had his fill

Now there are questions in this story
For those who leave their lambs
In the care of another one
Who is a hired hand
Do they have the heart of a shepherd?
Are they strong as they appear?
And do you know what they would do
When the wolf comes near?

O Great Shepherd, have mercy on the lives of my children. Help me as a parent be mindful of whom I ask to watch them. Give me a discerning heart. Open my eyes to make sure those I enlist to assist are trustworthy and brave. If they are found lacking, give me the courage to dismiss them and the wisdom to find others more worthy to help. In Jesus' mighty name. Amen.

56

Waking the Dawn

I will awaken the dawn.

PSALM 57:8

The alarm was set for four o'clock in the morning, and I slept confident that it would perform its important job of lifting me out of the depths of quiet slumber. I needed to be up at such an excruciating hour to cover the distance I had to travel that morning to make it into my deerstand before the appearance of the sun. However, I didn't contemplate a semi-truck mowing down a few power poles just up the road and bringing a screeching halt to the flow of electricity to our power panel.

Thankfully, something happened that helped the morning hunt take place after all. Somewhere deep in my psyche a wake-up buzzer must mysteriously exist. My eyes suddenly popped open, and I immediately saw darkness in the room. Assuming I had sleep time remaining, I turned to check the red numbers on my alarm clock. When I saw nothing but black, I realized right away there must be a power outage. When that shock hit me I instantly roused from my stupor. Nervous that I had slept longer than intended, I quickly pulled my wrist up close to my eyes and pushed the tiny light button on my Timex. When I saw the indigo-blue glow of 4:15, I relaxed and smiled as I drank in the relief that I was a mere 15 minutes behind schedule. I jumped up, quickly dressed, quietly grabbed my gear, and headed toward the wild. And the best part of all was that I would still be there well before sunrise.

As one who doesn't like to be late for sunup, and who is also a musician, there's a line in a passage of Scripture I particularly appreciate. David said in Psalm 57:8, "Awake my glory! [Poetically "glory" refers to the soul.] Awake, harp and lyre! I will awaken the dawn." Except for the fact that I don't carry my guitar to my deerstand, I feel a certain kinship with the psalmist when I sit looking toward an unlit horizon.

It is in those "up and at 'em early" times that I can say to the sun, "Get up—and do what you do! Rise and bring your welcome skill at disbursing the darkness and comforting me with your warmth. And by the way, light things up so I can see some animal action!"

There are also some advantages to rising early

enough to be in the woods before the world awakes. I feel like I'm getting a headstart on living another day…as if I'm adding time to my years. And even more importantly, being awake early enough to tell the dawn to "get up" means there's extra time to do what David did when he awakened the dawn with his music. In verse 9 he says, "I will give thanks to You, O Lord."

That morning I had a lot to be thankful for, including not oversleeping! I did give thanks…and just as it did for David, the dawn awoke. It was a wonderful time to be on a deerstand.

Thank You, O wonderful Creator, for all those times I have been and will be privileged to awaken the dawn while sitting in the midst of Your marvelous creation. May I never waste an opportunity to greet the sun with my thanks for Your Son. In His name I pray! Amen.

57

When I Hear that Train

I make mention of you always in my prayers.

ROMANS 1:9 NKJV

There is something strangely emotive about the sound of a passing train in the distance. The massive iron wheels that rumble over the rails create a rhythmic rumble and the forlorn sound of that unmistakable whistle have stirred many poet hearts through the years. The list of songs about trains is as long as...well...a train.

You can probably instantly sing along when you hear "Life Is a Mountain Railroad" (the Carter Family), "Chattanooga Choo Choo" (Glenn Miller), "Last Train to Clarksville" (The Monkees), "Wabash Cannonball" (Roy Acuff), and more recently, "Long Black Train" (Josh Turner). Though the titles of songs about trains that could be named are nearly endless, I admit I've added to the number myself. And if you're a deer hunter, you might be interested to know my train song was birthed on a deerstand.

One morning when I was hunting in Tennessee

on a farm located about two miles from a railroad track, I heard it. Just after sunrise the distant muffled sound of a locomotive rumbled through the area. I could also hear the random call of its melodic voice singing out fair warning of its presence to those tempted to test their fate at railroad street crossings.

Hearing the far-off tune of the wheels and whistle instantly reminded me of my mother. She and my father live less than a mile from the railroad tracks that weave through their small town in West Virginia. The sounds of the engines and cars clanking and the wailing whistles are something she hears often. Some in the area consider it an annoyance. My mother, however, hears the sound much differently. To her, it has become a cue to keep a promise she made several years ago to her two kids, her grandkids, and her great-grandkids.

That morning the idea came to me to lyrically document the special significance she attaches to the train's passing. I did so primarily for the sake of the fortunate ones blessed to receive the benefit of her pledge. But if you happen to live, work, play, or hunt within earshot of an active railroad track, maybe this lyric will cause the song of the locomotive to take on a new meaning...and purpose for you too.

When I Hear that Train

Whenever I hear that train it takes me back
To where my mother lives, near the railroad tracks
It was there that she told me a long time ago,
"Child, I want you to know...

"You can be sure as long as I'm around
Every time I hear that train coming through our town
I'm gonna bow my head and close my eyes
And I'm gonna lift my hands up to the sky...

"And pray for you
When I hear that train come through
I'll pray for you, that's what I'm gonna do
God's gonna hear your name
Every time I hear that train comin' through
I'll pray for you"

The time and the dreams took me away
From that little town—but it's still there today
And I'm thankin' God there ain't no rust upon those rails
And for the promise Mama made
And for God, who never fails

Jesus, I have no doubt that my journey in this life has been abundantly blessed through the enduring prayers of my mother. Please honor her devotion by granting her greatest desire for me and for those she faithfully mentions to You each day—that we may know and accept You as our Lord and Savior and opt to serve You every day. Let me ride the rails of Your grace until I arrive safely at home with You. In Christ's name I pray. Amen.

58

The Ant War

[Jesus said,] *My food is to do the will of Him who sent Me and to accomplish His work.*

JOHN 4:32

Springtime is a wonderful time of the year for deer hunters. Even though the beginning of a new hunting season is many weeks away, there are joys in the pre-summer days:

- The long winter is passed, evidenced by consistent warm temperatures.

- The chances of an acorn-killing frost plummets to nearly zero as the months progress.

- The planting of corn, soybeans, and other tasty harvest-time attractants is underway, hopefully keeping critters interested in sticking around.

- Fawns will soon be added to the herd, assuring good numbers of animals for the future.

- Early "therapeutic" scouting occurs for hunters itching to be in the woods. Deer movements are more easily determined because ground cover is heavier in the spring. Sharp deer hooves cut a more detectible trail so we can see where they rest and how they're moving from bedding areas to feeding spots.

- Last year's hunting gear at favorite sporting good stores is marked down even lower and yields significant savings.

While springtime does indeed provide hunters with much to appreciate and plenty to look forward to, there is one thing that happens then that can be a downright bummer. It's the time of year when a small critter bent on doing significant damage experiences significant population growth. That little pest is the mighty carpenter ant. And "mighty" is not a reference to their large size (in the ant world anyway). No, it's their corporate demolition potential.

A colony of carpenter ants can quickly take down deerstands of all sizes if they're made of wood. The ants don't eat the lumber, but they burrow into it and build their homes, tampering significantly with the integrity of the structure. Once the timbers are weakened, the stand becomes a very dangerous place to hang out...or crash to the ground, as the case may be. Unfortunately, there have been some who have unknowingly climbed into a stand before inspecting it closely. Crumpling under the hunter's weight, the result is usually injury, but for an unfortunate few it's been death.

One of the weapons used against the carpenter ant, as well as other members of the "formicidae" family, is a product designed to destroy them in a way that is most intriguing. I discovered its unusual characteristics as a result of my own battle against a tiny band of destroyers.

The product is a deadly mixture of sweetness and poison, and the instructions for using it are simple and pretty much hands off. While I would prefer stomping and spraying the insects when they come purely for the sake of revenge, the makers of this specific pest control product advise otherwise. They say to place containers of the substance in places where ants travel to and from their homes so they'll find it. Then we're to leave them alone so they'll eat it. The idea is for them to carry the poison back to the colony. The worker ants live long enough after consuming the toxin to make it back to their "galleries," and once they're "home," they pass the food or poison to their roommates before dying. Within a few days, hopefully, the entire colony begins to die.

Though there is a certain sadness felt for the tiny little ants and their family members who face such a cruel and tragic end, I appreciate the chemically based battle strategy that some unidentified genius came up with. Whoever he or she is, my camo hat is removed in his or her honor because the stuff really works.

In dealing with an infestation of ants, I realized that the scientist involved in creating the pesticides didn't just supply us with a tried-and-true way to combat ants. They also gave us a picture—a warning actually—that could save the spiritual lives of entire human families and their "colonies."

There is a lot of "moral poison" available outside our homes, such as half-truths, myths, and unholy "fables" (1 Timothy 4:7). The sources of these vary from the "attractive but spiritually toxic" information found in entertainment (TV, movies, video games, books, magazines) to the "sweet but lethal" humanistic philosophies often promoted in schools. Though it seems harmless at first, the noxious "mind food" that is consumed begins to affect the inner life of the carrier. Then, without knowing that it is happening, the spiritually damaging attitudes and ideas spread and infect others. Eventually the plague of untruths moves through the entire family and organization, and slowly the colony begins to weaken and eventually die.

An important question this ant war picture caused me to ask is one I hope you'll consider asking as well: "Have I...or am I...taking in anything that could bring spiritual or moral harm to me and those around me?" I ask myself this question often as a spiritual physical. How's your health these days?

God, I don't want to be the source of spiritual contamination for my family or church. Help me be careful regarding the food for the soul I consume and share. Thank You for providing the healthy nourishment found in the Bible. Increase my hunger for Your Word, and help me digest it for my good and the good of those around me. In Jesus' name I pray. Amen.

59

Gone Green

He makes me lie down in green pastures.

PSALM 23:2

I never dreamed I'd live to see the day that a color would define the hopes of the survival of our culture. But that day came to pass. We've "gone green." The basic message that flows in this current of color is that to keep the standard of quality at a high level in resources that include water, soil, and air, we humans must keep the impact of our presence (some call it our "carbon footprint") to a minimum. With more than four billion people now living on the planet, I concede that there's validity to activities such as recycling and finding cleaner-burning fuels. For the most part, the movement toward a green attitude is a good thing. I'm happy to report that as a deer hunter I'm onboard the emerald train.

Yes indeed. I bring good news to those who are on the frontlines of the green war. I am glad to report that hunters know more about the importance of green than nearly any other group. Green is critical to our lives. It means...

- the safety button is in the "on" position on our rifles, shotguns, pistols, and crossbows.

- if the deer looks right at us and calmly starts feeding again, the light and dark shades of olive in our camo pattern are working to full advantage.

- when the leaves turn green we're only five months or so away from opening day of archery season.

- envy...the green-eyed monster that inhabits the eyes of our buddies when they see the big one we bagged.

- after a shot, if a good amount of green ooze is mingled with a small amount of red blood on the ground or on a leaf, unfortunately it's a "gut shot." This requires extra effort and time to search for the wounded animal to end its suffering and fill your tag.

- if it's the color of mucus we're coughing up, there will be no hunting today... maybe.

- the green truck pulling us over has someone inside it who wants to check our license,
  equipment, and success in the woods.

- the color of cash that can get us new
  equipment!

While I'm jesting a bit about the hunter's affection
for the color green, I'm also offering a sincere defense
of a segment of our population that is often accused
of not caring about the planet. Some extremists argue
that no one should ever be allowed to hunt. But the
reality is that hunters are an incredibly important and
active part of animal and earth conservation.

Without hunters, animal populations can multiply exponentially, resulting in more assaults on food
crops. Thus it would be necessary to farm even more,
burning more fossil fuels as a result, and disturbing
more land (eliminating wilderness areas and forests).
Furthermore, without hunters, the increased number
of free-roaming animals would create more road haz-
ards. The increased numbers of vehicles wrecked in
these accidents would create the need to make more,
resulting in additional precious land being mined for
the ores to make the metal. And on and on the negative possibilities go if the deer hunter were removed
from the conservation picture. The huge increase in

wild game populations also could result in overgrazing (which could lead to starvation), rampant disease, and an out-of-balance ecosystem.

So yes, I'm green…because I'm part of the movement to take care of our planet. Count me in and pass the olive branches. Besides, being green puts me (and you!) in really good company. God is in favor of green! He "makes me lie down in *green* pastures" (Psalm 23:2). He says, "I gave the *green* plant" (Genesis 9:3). He even "directed [the disciples] to have all the people sit down in groups on the *green* grass" as He prepared to create an "energy and resource saving" meal by using five loaves of bread and two fish to feed 5000 people (Mark 6:39).

God likes green…and so do we!

Lord and Creator, thank You for the great green garden called earth. Show me ways I can help keep it healthy and clean. I worship and honor You, I want to be a good steward of what You've provided. In Your Son's name I pray. Amen.

60

Answers Require Questions

Ask and it shall be given to you.

Matthew 7:7

One of my favorite hunters, writers, and speakers is a gentleman named Jason. Trailing me on the path of time and hunting experience by approximately 15 years, the man has forgotten more about how to hunt than I've learned in my four decades of engaging in the fair chase. In addition to his impressive skills with bow, pen, and spoken word is a gift I quite honestly envy…at times in an almost sinful way. I learned about it while riding with him to a hunt on the back roads of the great state of Tennessee.

As we passed farm after farm he'd say, "I have permission to hunt there. Nice piece of property." Then he'd give some detail about it that only someone who had walked those specific woods would know. Going down the road a mile or two, driving past the next place, he'd start in again. "I can hunt there. Nice folks. The man and his wife are doctors, and they're not here a lot, but I have a key to the gate."

After nearly a dozen "They let me hunt there" reports, I finally asked the question that was burning in my blaze-orange brain: "How have you managed to garner all these places to hunt?"

Jason smiled and said, "Well, when I'm driving around an area and see deer in a field, I knock on some doors and find out who owns that piece of property. Once I learn who owns it, I seek out where they live. When I find them I ask for permission to hunt."

Jason's method of securing rights to hunt on land that belongs to total strangers is the embodiment of a very famous Bible passage. Matthew 7:7 records Jesus saying, "Ask, and it will be given you; seek, and you will find; knock, and it will be opened to you." With the verse comes a guarantee that it will yield results: "For everyone who asks receives, and he who seeks finds, and to him who knocks it will be opened" (verse 8).

As Jason and I passed yet another farm that he was allowed to hunt, I asked him another question: "Man, where do you get the courage to go up to these folks and knock on their doors? I just don't have that kind of nerve."

"What's there to be afraid of, Steve? They're either going to say yes or no. Besides, I figure they're not going to come to me and ask me to hunt their property. 'You have not 'cause you ask not.' The bottom line is that an answer requires a question... and I'm not afraid to ask it!"

Jason's kind of bravery and confident attitude is what we can all use when we go to the Lord in prayer, praising Him first and then presenting our needs. In fact, this level of trust honors God! If His answer to our request is "yes," we can proceed, knowing we needed to go through the door we knocked on. If He says "no," there's no harm done. God loves us and wants only the best for us, so if He says no we know what we requested isn't in His plan for us. We can smile and go on to the next "farm" (so to speak).

After a few rides with Jason in the Tennessee countryside and getting some of his back-roads tutoring on the Matthew 7:7 method, I'm better equipped to find more places to hunt. Plus, I'm praying with more confidence. Thanks, Jase!

Lord, You are a kind and caring Father who loves me enough to say yes as well as no. Thank You that I can confidently come to You in prayer, knowing You love me and want the best for me. I trust You. In Jesus' name. Amen.

61

East and West

*As far as the east is from the west, so far has
He removed our transgressions from us.*

There's a story about a fellow who was going to join a friend to hunt for the first time on a farm in a neighboring state. Having never been in that area, he asked his buddy to send a map. The drawing that was provided was not to scale, nor did it have sufficient landmarks to help him easily locate the farm. After arriving in the general vicinity and driving around and around the countryside in search of the right entry gate, he reluctantly conceded that it was time to get some help. He looked ahead and saw a farmer working along the road on a fence line. He pulled up to the stranger, rolled his truck window down, and humbly made his inquiry.

"Excuse me, sir. Uh, excuse me!"

The farmer turned around, slid his pliers into his overalls, and walked toward the car, wiping his hands on a red hankie that he took out of his back pocket.

"Yes, sir. May I help you?"

"Well, I'm sort of lost, I guess you could say. I'm trying to meet up with a friend of mine to hunt this week, and I was hoping you could tell me where the entry to Mr. Gardner's property is."

The farmer leaned in and began to answer slowly. First he pointed to the driver's right.

"Well, sir, if you go east, which is that way, the Gardners' gate is about 24,000 miles. If you miss it, just keep driving, and you'll go right back by it."

Then he pointed to the inquirer's left and said, "But if you go that way, which is west, it's about a mile and half down the road. If you miss it, just keep driving and you'll come right back to it."

There was momentary stillness in the hunter's truck as he assimilated the information. Suddenly he broke out into a belly laugh. The farmer then knew his joke had worked one more time.

I'll admit that after hearing that story I've had some fun with folks who have stopped and asked me for directions. If they're close to where they need to be and I know where to send them, I use the farmer's "method." It's amusing to watch their faces as the joke slowly sinks in. Most "victims" eventually laugh, but some look at me like I have barbed wire coming out my ears. Sadly, a few of them scratch their citified heads and drive away...still lost.

If you think about the imagery in the farmer's east/west picture you'll find an amazing truth. What he was implying, whether he knew it or not, was that east is always east and west is always west. It's not like what happens when you go north or south. If you go south, for example, you will eventually start going north, and vice versa. On the other hand, if you go east, you'll be forever heading east. My mind almost started emitting smoke as the gears of comprehension ground through the full impact of the profound difference in the two sets of directions.

A well-known passage of Scripture that came to my mind is likely the same one you're thinking of at this moment: "As far as the east is from the west, so far has He removed our transgressions from us."

What an absolutely brilliant way to comfort all of us who have placed our trust in God, through Christ, for redemption from our sins. The very thought that just as God separated east from west, He completely separates sin from the sinners is more than an astounding analogy...it's the best news I've ever heard!

God, thank You for forgiving me. I'm so glad You send me in one direction and my sin in another! And thank You for doing this for me each time I come to You to confess the burden of a transgression. In Jesus' name I pray. Amen.

62

Finish Well

*You have need of endurance, so that when you
have done the will of God,
you may receive what was promised.*

HEBREWS 10:36

The old fellow stood at the fence and looked longingly at the huge deer that had just jumped it and now stood broadside while staring at him. As if tempting him to shoot, the buck stood there for what seemed like forever and then ran away at the sight of a fast-approaching hunter.

"Why didn't you take the shot, Gramps? You had every chance in the world!" the young hunter asked.

The seasoned hunter didn't respond immediately to his grandson's challenge. He remained motionless, looking toward the ghost of the monstrous whitetail... the one that got away. Then he spoke softly. "Boy, you know me better than that. And you know very well that the land on the other side of this fence is off limits to our family. Old Man Terrell would have us for supper if he caught us over there."

The heavy breathing of the winded grandson grew very quiet as his grandfather continued. "Young man, I've been around for a lot of years and managed to build a pretty good reputation for being on the up-and-up when it comes to following the rules. I'm not about to let an old buck tempt me into messing up now. I'm too close to the end of my season for such foolishness. I hope you'll remember what I'm telling you."

With that, the two of them turned and headed for the grandfather's house. No shots were fired that day, but a great harvest took place in the boy's heart. He learned firsthand what integrity looks like. If he imitated what was personified in the life of his gramps, the young man would do well in and out of the woods.

Another young grandson gleaned a similar picture of greatness in his grandfather. Here's their story.

Finish Well

He'll turn eighty-one next Sunday
I called him on the phone
I said, "I'm coming to see you, Grandpa

What can I bring along?
Would you like a dish for your TV or
Would you like the Internet?"
He said, "Thank you, boy, but this ain't the time
To be tripping over stuff like that 'cause…

"I want to finish well
I want to end this race
Still leaning on
His amazing grace
I want my last few miles to testify
That God never fails
I don't want to fall down this close to the line
I want to finish well."

He said, "You can bring me a Bible
Where the words are big and tall
So these old eyes can read the truth
That will help me not to fall!"

Both grandfathers in these stories handed down incredibly valuable examples to their grandsons. Their determination has become mine too. I want to live according to the passage in Hebrews that these two old gents have chosen to live by: "Let us also lay aside every encumbrance and the sin which so easily entangles us [including really big deer], and let us run with endurance the race that is set before us, fixing our eyes on Jesus [and not vanities such as worthless entertainment], the author and perfecter [finisher] of faith" (12:1-2). May it be so for us all.

God, I am thankful for those among us who have endured their years with integrity. I pray for Your help to do the same so that my life can be an example of the strength You provide...the kind that is needed to finish well. In Jesus' name I pray. Amen.

63

The Invitation

*Proclaim the excellencies of Him who has
called you out of darkness into
His marvelous light.*

1 Peter 2:9

Perhaps five of the sweetest words any deer hunter can ever hear are "Come hunt on my farm!" Absolute joy courses through the mind and heart of this passionate pursuer of the whitetail when an invitation like this is extended. Thankfully I've been on the receiving end of those treasured words a few times. One of those invitations took place within a five-minute drive of my home.

My wife, Annie, and I had moved to the rural area just a week or two earlier. We were walking a back road to enjoy the area and learn the territory. As we strolled down the narrow lane we saw an approaching couple. When we met, I spoke up.

"Hello! We're new to the area. We're Steve and Annie Chapman. What's your name, and where do you live?"

We learned their names were Rick and Cindy, and that we were standing within eyeshot of their house that sat on the edge of 40 wooded acres.

Cindy asked, "And what do you all do?"

We gave an overview of our "traveling musicians and writers" life and then I added, "Along with our work as singers, I just recently finished my first book for hunters called *A Look at Life from a Deer Stand.*"

Cindy's facial expression instantly turned from a smile to a sort of pensive look as she said, "So you're a deer hunter, huh?"

I worriedly thought, *Oh no! She's not a fan of hunting, and I've just offended her in a big-time way!*

Then, much to my relief, she spoke the nicest words any neighbor could ever say.

"We can't keep anything in our garden because of the deer around here. They eat nearly everything we plant. Is there any way you could come and eliminate some of them for us?"

Rick smiled and heartily nodded his agreement.

I think I heard a full orchestra play and a choir of angels sing! And it wasn't just because I realized I wasn't going to get beaten with the rod of radical environmental verbiage. It was also because I was asked to serve my neighbors in such a wonderful way. A feller just doesn't get an invitation like that every day.

As it turns out, Rick and Cindy's acreage became one of my most frequented retreats. With the closeness of their farm, the freedom to appear anytime unannounced (they know my truck), and the plentiful game on their property, it's hard to count the mornings and evenings spent there "helping" my friends.

Any serious deer hunter who doesn't own property to hunt understands why Cindy and Rick's offer to let me help them "keep their garden safe" remains high on the list of my most valued invitations. But it doesn't occupy first place. That spot is reserved for the invitation the following lyric explains.

The Invitation

He met me at the door of the world where I'd been
    hiding
He said, "Come on in." His eyes were so inviting
He looked past my outside, straight into my heart
And when I went inside, I stepped out of the dark

Into the light, lost to found
Death to life, no longer bound
By the chains that held me to my sin
O bless the day He invited me in!

An invitation so rich with mercy
To a soul so sad and poor
O what joy I found when I went walking
Through Christ, the Open Door

Into the light, lost to found
Death to life, no longer bound
By the chains that held me to my sin
O bless the day He invited me in!

I accepted God's call to come to Him through Christ more than 30 years ago, and I'm eternally glad I did! The good news is that the invitation to come out of the dark woods (or streets) of sin and step into the light of God's saving grace is extended to everyone. Will you accept it?

Father in heaven, thank You for reaching out to me with Your gentle grace and saying to my heart, "Come to Me and live in My light." I accept the invitation You sent through Your Son, Jesus Christ. He is my Lord and Savior who died and rose again to free me from sin and draw me close to You. In His name I thank You! Amen.

64

The Web

The hope of the godless will perish, whose confidence is fragile, and whose trust a spider's web.

JOB 8:13-14

I hadn't hunted the woods where my friend was taking me. We arrived well before daylight, and in the darkness I randomly choose a tree that seemed to be a good spot for a ground blind. With plans to sit on a fold-out, three-legged stool, it was a bit of a challenge to find a place in the low light that would provide enough foliage for cover and some open shooting lanes. Dawn finally arrived, and I was quite pleased with where I ended up. The spot needed a minimal amount of trimming with my hand-held clippers to get ready for the hopeful ambush of a deer.

As the rising sunlight filtered through the canopy of leaves above me, I was excited about being in a new place. There's something about being in unfamiliar territory that adds an extra degree of anticipation to my hunts. To add to the enjoyment, there was a beauty about the way the woods responded to the gradual dawn that made the morning even more spectacular. Like extremely slow lightning bolts, sun-rays were shooting through the trees, lighting up the forest floor, and wrapping some of the tree trunks in a golden-reddish hue.

As I took in the visual treat of morning scenery, I noticed that a spotlight sunbeam was coming across my back. The subtle warmth felt good in the early fall chill. I closed my eyes, took in a deep breath, and gloried in the moment. When I opened my eyes I saw it.

The brilliant sunlight reflected off a single strand of a spider's web that was stretched taut between the trunks of two young saplings I was using for cover. The web was moving, as if responding to a gentle breeze, but there was no wind that morning. I was puzzled by its bouncing motion until I saw the reason. A spider was at one end laboring away.

I was privileged to observe the expert weaver's work from nearly the beginning of the process. As I was admiring how efficient, quick, and precise the web was coming together, it dawned on me that I had my video camera. Slowly I retrieved it and started filming. I knew the window of sunlight would even-tually close, and I wanted to get as much of the tiny architect's work as I could. I continued to watch the web through my eyepiece. The well-lit close-up I was enjoying was breathtaking. Strand by delicate strand the intricate web was formed. As it danced under the micro-weight of the busy worker's movements it sparkled in the sunlight. I was willing to use the entire tape and all my battery power to document the entire build. Sadly, the sun traveled on and the beaming stage light turned off.

I have no idea if any...or how many...deer may have walked by while my eyes were engaged in the spider's incredible show. I wasn't about to turn away from the amazing structure the many-legged engineer was creating. In fact, I didn't see a single deer that morning. But in no way was the sit a loss. I got memorable footage of the work of one of nature's most gifted architects (that I can show to grandkids someday), and I carried out of the woods the motivation to find out what the tiny scene could teach me.

When I got home I went to the concordance in the back of my Bible and looked up the words "spider" and "web." Though not mentioned many times in the Scriptures, there are at least two images that spiders and webs yield. One is interesting; the other is sobering.

In Proverbs 30:28 NKJV, the spider is on the short list of four things on the earth that are small but exceedingly wise. "The spider skillfully grasps with its hands, and it is in kings' palaces." What an inspiring picture of how insignificance can be an advantage if used wisely. Examples of this truth have been displayed many times throughout history, but one example that immediately comes to my mind is how many employees who started as backroom janitor-types quietly fed on the knowledge of a company's operation and ended up either owning that business or successfully creating an improved version of it.

The second reference highlights the spider's web. Job 8:14 reads, "Whose confidence is fragile, and whose trust a spider's web." Wondering what this verse meant, I did what is very often required to understand it. I backed up and read the previous verse. Connected, the two passages read, "So are the paths of all who forget God; and the hope of the godless will perish, whose confidence is fragile and whose trust a spider's web."

What could be more undependable for a lean-to than a fragile spider's web? As wonderful as they are to look at and to marvel at their complex beauty, they are worthless supporters of anything heavier than a fly or other tiny bug. The same is true for our lives. When our hope is placed in anything other than God, disappointment will be certain.

Let's not put our trust in attractive-yet-fragile things such as talents, wealth, brain power, social position, or even a false sense of innocence. All these are flimsy spider webs, so to speak, and do not deserve our full confidence.

God, I want to put the full weight of my confidence in You. Help me to never fall into the trap of trusting anything in this life other than You. In Your Son's name I pray. Amen.

65

Benny and Joe

It is appointed for men...

GENESIS 3:19

Benny & Joe

Benny and Joe were old friends
They both loved the game of baseball
They filled those seats behind home plate
From early spring till late fall
Then one day Benny's heart got tired
For him the game of life was over
And Joe told him as they said goodbye
"Get us good seats over yonder."

Well the home team was back in town
And the weather it was sunshine
But Joe couldn't bear that empty seat
So he was on his porch at game time
When all at once in his front yard
There stood his best friend, Benny
Joe jumped up and said, "Ol' Buddy,
We can catch the last five innings."

Benny said, "Joe, I can't stay long
I just came back to tell you
There's baseball up in heaven
But that's not all the good news.
They got me playing shortstop
Like I dreamed someday I would do
And I just thought you'd like to know, Joe
You'll be pitching Thursday."

This lyric is my rendition of a story our preacher told as he began a Sunday-morning sermon. When he finished the tale, and after the laughter subsided in the sanctuary, he looked at the congregation and continued,

Of course I can't say that the theology in this story is accurate, but I think you get the point. The truth is, in a room this size filled with this many people, the possibility that someone among us could be called up to pitch this coming Thursday is pretty good. The question is, "Are you ready to take the mound?"

Then he punctuated the reality of the truth by tenderly quoting Hebrews 9:27: "It is appointed for men to die once and after this comes judgment."

The room was silent as we pondered what had just been said. Each of us knew the preacher was absolutely right…and everyone quietly wondered who should be the one to head to the local baseball diamond and warm up the old arm.

The sobering reality of the truth in the pastor's sermon followed me home that Sunday. It also followed me into the woods the next day when I got up before sunrise and headed to the deerstand. With the story of Benny and Joe still fresh on my mind, I decided it would be wise to spend some time saying thanks to God for the provisions of His grace and the forgiveness for my sins that comes through Jesus Christ. It was also a good opportunity to offer up a prayer that He would help me always be ready for the inevitable "appointment." What motivated me to pray that way? It was Monday…and Thursday was only a few days away!

Lord, thank You for the reminders that there is a day coming when I will leave the woods of this life and enter the field of eternity. Help me be ready for that day. It is by the grace of Jesus Christ…and in His name I pray. Amen.

66

Dancers and Singers

Let the field exult…then all the trees of the forest
will sing for joy before the LORD.

Of the endless and glorious sights to enjoy in the
great outdoors, few match the fluid beauty of
a field of grain or tall grass as it sways in the wind.
Seeing the wispy tops of the fragile, knee-high stalks
as they bend in wavelike unison is, without exception,
one of nature's most graceful shows to watch.

I've been blessed to be sitting in tree stands near
open fields when the wind showed up to dance with
the grain. I've nearly had to catch my breath at times
when, from the advantage of an elevated perch, I've
been privileged to see the elegant display of the invisible touching the visible. And more than once I've
thought of the classic song "America the Beautiful"
and its description of "amber waves of grain." The
poem was written by Katharine Lee Bates. I wonder
where she was when she penned those words?

As I was reading Psalm 96, the familiar and

delightful image of a waving field of grain came to mind. The first half of verse 12 says, "Let the field exult, and all that is in it." What a beautiful thought—that the windswept grain is a picture of rejoicing. From the moment I read that portion of the passage and connected exultation with the swaying motion of a tall grassy field, I've never wondered again why I experience such joy and peace at the sight of it. But as they say in the commercials, "But wait! There's more!"

When I continued reading and came to the second line, a new and exciting addition to the wind and grain field picture was revealed. "Then all the trees of the forest will sing for joy before the LORD."

Yes! I've heard the trees singing…and you have too if you've been in the woods when the wind kicks up. Remember the rustling, hissing sound that rises and falls in volume with the varying intensity of the wind (and makes it tough to hear walking deer)? The currents of air flowing through thousands of leaves cause them to sway back and forth, softly colliding and gently scraping against each other. That sound I now think of as joyful singing.

There's one other interesting imagery in this verse I'd like to point out. "*Let* the field exult, and all that is in it. *Then* all the trees of the forest *will* sing for joy."

Notice the subtle "if this happens, that will happen next" progression.

In nature, that which is lower, humble, more exposed, and more vulnerable has the grand opportunity to influence the greater, less approachable, more imposing figures. When the wind arrives, the tender shoots of grain in the field begin to happily wave in the presence of the unseen, and soon the wind ripples into the woods and the nearby forest will sing. And when that happens they become a team of dancers and singers. And what is the purpose of this corporate display of joy? Ah...verse 13 holds the answer. It's joy and exultation in a momentous announcement: "*Let* the field exult, and all that is in it. *Then* all the trees of the forest *will* sing for joy before the LORD, for *He is coming.*"

There are likely more insights that can be drawn from verses 12 and 13, but one I appreciate is how the imagery has changed the way I think about my potential as a living stalk in the grain field called the Church of the Living God. If I am willing to join other believers, and we all respond to the effect of the movement of the wind we know as the Holy Spirit, we can influence those whom we consider high-profile types in our lives. Employers, government officials, celebrities, world leaders, professors, and others who are influential among us can be rightly reminded that "Jesus is coming."

So I say, "Let us exult in the Spirit so that it comes to pass that 'all the trees in the forest will sing for joy!'" Their singing should be the goal of our dancing. May this always be true!

Father in heaven, thank You for the breeze of the Holy Spirit, who comes and causes me to rejoice in knowing You. Help me to be faithful to happily report to the forest of the world the marvelous news of Your soon-to-come arrival. Amen.

67

Follow the Blood

In Him we have redemption through His blood,
the forgiveness of our trespasses,
according to the riches of His grace.

EPHESIANS 1:7

One of the most profoundly emotional moments for me as a deer hunter comes not when the animal is spotted or when it walks into the shooting range of my bow or gun, but after I take the shot. When I leave my hiding place and approach my arrow that might be sticking in the ground or when I go to the spot where the deer was standing when the gun was fired, a mysteriously unique and spirit-deep rush washes over me. It's the moment when I see the first drop or splatter of blood.

As I search the area for more of the liquid tell-tale sign that my shot connected and the life of the animal is fleeing, I can feel my eyes widen, my pulse rate climb, and my breathing noticeably quicken. As I find each drop or pool of blood, I can hear my voice, "There…and…there…ah…here…more…yes…yes!"

Finding first blood is a highly charged discovery.

And even though it's happened many times through the years, it never ever gets old. My most recent finding of wound blood included something totally unexpected. It was, for lack of a better word, a revelation. I envisioned a picture I hadn't seen before.

After a few days of mulling over what came to me while on that trail of blood, I decided to put the epiphany in a song.

Follow the Blood

I watched the arrow as it flew
From the shelf upon my bow
I was quite sure its flight was true
When I saw the red stains in the snow

So I follow the blood
That crimson sign
Follow that trail
I know I'll find
The death that gives life
A gift from above
Sadness and joy
Follow the blood

I saw the drops of sorrow on the ground
And at once it came to me
The hope of all mankind is found
On the way to Calvary

So I follow the blood
That crimson sign
Follow that trail
I know I'll find
The death that gives life
A gift from above
Sadness and joy
Follow the blood

O merciful and loving Father, I offer my sincere thanks to You for the gift of the sacrifice of Your only begotten Son. The shedding of His blood, I know, is my only hope for atonement for my sins. I accept Your eternally generous gift and will testify always that it is Jesus' blood alone that cleanses me from unrighteousness. In His name I pray. Amen.

68

Grease Is Cheaper

Preserve the unity of the Spirit.

Ephesians 4:3

Fifteen miles from my driveway is one of my favorite places on the planet to hunt. It is a couple hundred acres that has a perfect combination of thickets, meadows, water, and crops. It's owned by a gentleman, friend, and lifelong farmer named Joe.

One day while talking with Joe about the details required to keep a farm efficiently running he said something I've never forgotten. We were specifically discussing the many pieces of machinery he used and the massive amounts of effort and cash required for their upkeep. He looked across the bed of my truck, grinned at me, and said as he pointed toward the barn filled with working implements, "There's one thing I've learned with these old tractors and their attachments. If I'm going to salvage my time and money, I have to remember that grease is cheaper than metal."

I'd never heard that statement, but the point was

immediately understood and well taken. Since that day, nearly every time I think of something that I should do to keep a piece of my equipment in good working order, I think of Joe's words. His profound quip comes to my mind when I'm squirting grease in my mower spindles or changing the oil in my motorcycle. Without a doubt, the truth of his advice is applicable to any situation where there are moving metallic parts.

But Joe's wisdom goes beyond the world of mowers and tractors. It reaches into the everyday matters of life and relationships.

Think about marriage maintenance. If we fail to take care to communicate with each other regularly and often, sooner or later the gears of love might grind and splinter. If that happens, the price needed to repair the emotional damage can be high.

Consider our roles as parents. If we let day after day go by and don't frequently offer confirming words of encouragement to our kids, eventually the hefty cost for rehab and counseling will have to be paid. And in our relationships with extended family, if we constantly ignore them, there'll come a time when the friction could cause irreparable damage.

Joe's wisdom also applies to the spiritual family we call the church. The apostle Paul offers an admonition regarding the maintenance of the harmony among the saints: "[Be] diligent to preserve [or maintain] the unity of the Spirit in the bond of peace" (Ephesians 4:3). Thankfully, Paul didn't give such a significant instruction to the church and leave the members without a solution or instructions. The "grease" Paul instructed the believers to use to effectively care for unity was addressed in verses 1 and 2: "I...implore you to walk in a manner worthy of the calling with which you have been called, with all humility and gentleness, with patience, showing tolerance for one another in love."

It's hard to imagine a better lubricant for church relationships than what Paul suggested. And what will maintain the body of Christ will also surely help keep a family in good working condition. There are two critical questions to ask: Are we careful to apply Paul's advice? And do we do so often? If we don't do it at home and in the pews, there will come a day when everything will come to a grinding halt.

Thank You, Father, for the oil of Your love that You've given me to help preserve my relationships with others. Please remind me often to apply it at home and in Your house. In Jesus' name. Amen.

69

I Wanna Go with My Daddy

He guides me in the paths of righteousness.

PSALM 23:3

It was a heart-wrenching sight to see when my buddy and I pulled out of his driveway and looked back. There in the driveway, resting in his mother's arms, was a little boy dressed in camo pajamas with one of the saddest faces I've ever seen. Tears were streaming down his tender face as he watched his dad head off to hunt without him.

My friend tentatively pressed the gas pedal and looked over at me with a pained expression. "Ouch!" was all he could grunt out. After a moment or two of gathering his composure, he said, "The minute his mama says its okay for him to go, he'll be in this truck with me."

That little boy in the driveway was living proof of an age-old fact. There is an amazing and mysterious longing that most children have that makes them want to go where they see their dads go. It seems, for example, there are countless kids who observed the vocational direction their fathers took and have chosen to follow in their footsteps. Think about it. Do the Andretti boys drive race cars? Are the Bush boys in politics? How many of the Graham kids are in ministry? Just how many more Manning boys are there who can throw footballs?

If children seem to have such a draw to follow the paths their fathers walked, does it not behoove us men to consider carefully where we're going? And is this not true especially when it comes to where we are headed in terms of eternity? It is a sobering thought that one day down the road of time we'll turn around to see that the moral and spiritual steps we placed on the sands of our years are the very tracks our kids will follow.

Do you need to reconsider the direction you're going in light of the possibility that it will be the same destination your kids head toward? There's a father in Texas named Herman who would agree, and it was his nephew in Alabama who told me about his uncle's change of ways. Herman's story is in this song I share in my concerts:

I Wanna Go with My Daddy

He hid behind his Sunday morning paper
His little boy behind a box of Cheerios

She poured some coffee and thought about the
   church
Where their family never goes
And when she brought it up he said,
"I won't be goin', I guess I'm headed
To the place made for folks like me."
Then she asked their little boy across the table
"Would you like to go to church with me?"
And he said...

"I wanna go with my daddy
To the place he said is made for him
That's what I wanna do
'Cause I love my daddy and wherever he's goin'
I wanna go there too!"

Well...he never heard any words that cut him deeper
And he couldn't hide the tears on his face
She said, "If we hurry we can make it!"
He had a change of destination on that day

Now they can sing "Amazing Grace" together
And he can smile when he hears his little boy say...

"I wanna go with my daddy
To the place he said is made for him
That's what I wanna do
'Cause I love my daddy and wherever he's goin'
I wanna go there too!"

I say a personal congratulations to Herman for being brave enough to change the course of his life in such a powerful and profound way. He's a worthy example for any of us who want to plot a good and godly course for our kids.

God, give me the courage as a parent to take an honest look at the destination my heart is headed. I ask this for my good, and also for the eternal welfare of my kids. Guide me in the paths of righteousness for Your name's sake. May the aim of my family's journey always be You! In Jesus' name. Amen.

70

Jack

*Who knows what is good for a
man during his lifetime?*

ECCLESIASTES 6:12

Jack

Did you hear about Jack?
Let me tell you about it.
That thing he's always wanted
Today he finally got it
Year after year you know he tried and tried
But he wouldn't give up
He wouldn't be denied

This is the day we will all remember
This is the day when it all came together...for Jack
He finally broke the chains that held him back

Why he wanted what he got
Was never clear to most of us
Still he gave everything

He gave his blood and guts
But Jack answered that one question
That's always been on my heart
Just what does happen when a dog...
Finally catches the car?

This is the day we will all remember
This is the day when it all came together...for Jack
He finally broke the chains that held him back
Goodbye, Jack, you finally broke the chains that held
    you back.

Through my years of hunting, dogs have both helped and hindered my hunts. A few times I've heard dogs barking in the distance, and they've unknowingly caused fleeing deer to move into my stand area. In those cases the canines received my quiet thanks. But more often dogs have been guilty of ruining my hunts. Still, I have a deep affection for man's best friend. For that reason, the news of a demise of a dog like Jack brings with it a strange mixture of emotions.

My feelings range from sincere sorrow about his life of chained confinement to the momentary joy of knowing he was running free. Then I move to the total sadness that he's gone. I'll never get to pet his head and tell him how regretful I was to learn of his misfortune. I wish I could somehow tell him that his life and death taught me an important lesson.

With a similar intensity to what Jack showed in his constant desire to catch a passing car, there was one thing I passionately wanted. But, like Jack, I had no idea that what I wanted would not be a good thing for me to get. I shudder to think what would have happened if I'd managed to break the chain of restraint. Today I would either not be around or, at best, I would not be enjoying the life God has granted me.

I suppose you're wondering what I'm talking about…and it would certainly add more interest and drama if I named what I'd been chasing. But it's just too personal. Instead, why not put yourself and the object of your desire into this story? If you do this, I can say from experience that there are a couple of important questions to ask and answer:

- Is the thing you "bark" for each time you see or think of it something that will do you good?

- Does the object of your desire represent the demise of your physical, spiritual, mental, or financial life?

Jack didn't know to ask and answer these

questions...he was a dog. But *we* know better...or at least we should. Ask God to give you the courage to evaluate your desires and the discernment to know whether to work toward them or not. Also ask Him to strengthen the chains of your limitations if the thing you want most can cause harm.

God, thank You that You know what is best for me. If the thing(s) I desire are not the craving You've put in my heart, please reinforce the merciful chains of obedience and help me heed Your wisdom. In Jesus' name I pray. Amen.

71

Just Two Words

Well done good and faithful servant.

MATTHEW 25:21

Men, for the most part, don't require the use of a lot of words to believe they've sufficiently communicated. We can be avid fans of brevity when it comes to receiving and relaying messages. This propensity is especially revealed in our great enjoyment of how much information can be packed into a few words in the limited space of bumper stickers. A few of my personal favorites are:

- "I love cats too…let's share recipes!"
- "I'm low on estrogen, and I have a gun."
- "We haul milk on weekends" (seen on a septic tank truck).

Note that these stickers have an average of seven words each. The truth is that most men have an uncanny ability to enjoy communication with even fewer words. For many of us, two is plenty. Think about all the times we speak and hear volumes with just two linked words:

- "Nice shot" (a golfer's verbal novel about his buddy's skill).
- "That'll play" (a golfer's verbal novel about his buddy's lack of skill).
- "Tagged out" (a turkey hunter's memoir of his 45-day season).
- "Harley Davidson" (a mental 80-volume series about adventure).
- "I do" (a man's entire future summed up).

I suppose the list of word pairs that can satisfy a man's communication requirements is endless. But there are two words I'm looking forward to hearing that will gratify and please me beyond all else I'm sure. They were first heard by the faithful servants featured in the "talents" story found in Matthew 25. Because the servants increased their master's money by investing it while he was on a journey, they were commended for their wise management. The master said, "Well done."

Someday I will stand before God to hear His assessments of how I managed the gifts He's so graciously given me. In that moment I will be more than satisfied to hear those same two words that the servants heard. God's "Well done, Steve" will bring incredible joy—more joy than all other words spoken in my lifetime.

Lord, thank You for the gifts You've entrusted to me. I ask You for the wisdom to know how to multiply the gifts. Help me follow through for Your honor so I'll hear You tell me, "Well done" when I meet You face-to-face. In Your Son's name I pray. Amen.

72

We Saw the Evidence

Jesus wept.

JOHN 11:35

I'm not a fan of crying, but it's not for a reason
that has to do with a fear of appearing less manly.
Instead, my resistance to being reduced to tears has
a physical cause. When I cry (the way I did when my
dog died), my air passages restrict, which causes my
breathing to become uncomfortably labored. Even
worse, if I have to speak in the midst of the process,
the convulsing is downright embarrassing. So when
it comes to blubbering, I do everything I can possibly do to avoid it.

While I always prefer unrestricted air flow over a
good sob, I readily admit I'm a bit envious of those
who can bawl with abandon. One reason I wish I
could "let go" is motivated by the dread that Annie's
words might someday come true. On more than
one occasion (some sad and some happy) she's said,
"Steve, if you don't cry, you're gonna have a heart
attack. Even Jesus, the greatest and strongest among

us, knew how to cry!" She's referring to the shortest verse in the Bible where it's reported that "Jesus wept" in response to Lazarus' death (John 11:30-38).

Unfortunately, being a "rarely if ever" crier, even if it is for physiological reasons, may send the wrong message to others. I fear that my infrequent episodes of dam breakage might make me appear unfeeling and uncaring. While I can see that people could get that impression, it is not an accurate assessment. To the contrary—like all guys—I really do have feelings. They just don't turn to liquid often.

The people who have most noticed my ineptness as a tear dropper, besides my wife, have been our children. More than once they've commented on the fact that they've hardly ever seen tears on my face. Though I'm not totally sure, I think they've had an ongoing competition to see if they can do or say something that will "make the old man cry." Though some of their attempts have yielded some noticeable moisture (letters, gifts, public accolades), so far my tear valve is yet to be fully opened. When it does happen, it could very well become "breaking news," like it did for the family in the following rendition of their story.

Daddy Cried

I called my brother out in Idaho
I said, "It's about Daddy—we think you ought to know
It happened last night as the sun was going down
We were all out on the front porch watching our little
    town.

"Daddy said, 'If you have the time, there's something on
    my heart.'
Sissy looked at me, we both swallowed hard.
He started talking about his life and how blessed he'd
    been
And if it ever happened before, we can't remember
    when…

"Daddy cried
We saw the tears
Daddy cried
After all these years
We saw the evidence
He's soft inside
Tears don't lie,
Daddy cried.

"He talked about his job in the mines and how it fed
    us kids
How many times he could have died there, but he
    never did

And how he wished that Grandpa knew just how good
    he'd done
But how proud he was when he thought about his
    daughter and his sons...

"As he talked he could see that Mama had a worried
    look
He put his hand on hers, and said, 'I'm okay, its not time
    to close the books.
I just want to testify about how good God has been.'
That's when we saw it—that quiver on his chin...

"Daddy cried
We saw the tears
Daddy cried
After all these years
We saw the evidence
He's soft inside
Tears don't lie,
Daddy cried.
Just thought you'd like to know...
Daddy cried."

The part of this story that especially captured my
attention was how many years passed before the dad
revealed his tender side. It sounds too familiar! I never
did know what motivated him to suddenly let his
emotions be so unguarded. My best guess is that the

floodgates might have been opened by the disturbing news that his closest hunting buddy contracted a life-threatening disease. Whatever the reason, to hear that he broke the norm and openly spoke of the blessings of his life was inspiring. Knowing that a fellow non-crier was brave enough to let the evidence of his deep gratitude flow from his heart to his eyes is encouragement for me to do the same.

God, in Your wisdom You made rivers. Some are mighty enough to cut through the roughness and rocks of our great land. And though they bring life to those who live near it, they can be treacherous to navigate. And some rivers are smaller and quieter, designed to flow softly down a cheek, sometimes to bring healing and at other times to testify to joy. I pray for the grace and wisdom to fully understand that salty stream— the power of it—and to have the courage to let it flow. In Jesus' name. Amen.

73

Hunting on Credit

For this reason you also must be ready;
for the Son of Man is coming at an hour
when you do not think He will.

MATTHEW 24:44

In a letter from a fellow hunter from the state of Georgia named Gary, an interesting phrase was used that he said was coined by his dad. Gary wrote, "Steve, have you ever forgotten to bolt a shell in the chamber after you climbed up in your stand? You sit there *hunting on credit* and don't even realize it till you start to climb down!"

What an intriguing way to describe the error of assuming the "ammo bank" is full when in reality it's empty. And the answer to Gary's question, in a semi-funny way, is yes. Just a couple of years earlier it happened to me while on a hunt in a nearby county.

The field I wanted to monitor was a long, narrow plot the deer were enjoying that fall. One side was edged with woods about 10 yards deep before dropping off quickly into a ravine. The opposite side had a fence row that spanned the length of the field. Precisely in the middle of the long row was a break in the fence where a metal gate once hung. The deer favored the ease of the eight-foot passage from field to field, and there were plenty of tracks to prove it. I decided the best place for my climber was near the old gate posts.

The problem I encountered during setup was that there wasn't a single tree near the opening that was straight and suitable for my two-piece style of climber.

Still, I was determined to hunt that specific spot. I settled for a tree that required some fancy maneuvering of my stand around sizable knots, as well as extra effort to negotiate annoying crooks in the trunk. After what seemed hours (but was really about 20 minutes) of sweat-producing management, my climber was hanging on the tree, and I was high enough off the ground and felt sufficiently safe to sit down and enjoy the hunt.

I was quite sure that the evening would yield at least a sighting and maybe even a shot, but my dreams weren't fulfilled. As the sun began its westward journey beyond the horizon, I decided it was time to dismount and head home. The first thing I did, like any smart hunter does, was unload my weapon. That evening I was hunting with my .357 Magnum pistol. When I tilted the cylinder out to empty it, I couldn't believe what I saw. Nothing! Not one bullet!

As I sat there laughing at myself I realized I'd gotten so distracted with getting my tree stand positioned in the gnarly tree that I'd completely overlooked the last step in the set-up process: load the gun. Basically I'd spent the evening doing exactly what Gary's dad called "hunting on credit." I thought I was fully prepared for the moment of hunting fruition, when in reality I'd fallen majorly short of total readiness.

I have a feeling Gary and I aren't alone in making this mistake. And if we're blessed to continue to head to the woods for future hunts, it's not inconceivable that it might happen again.

As brothers in faith, Gary and I agree on a more important matter of readiness that we know is far more critical than merely making sure we load our hunting weapons. We've seen the warning in Matthew 24:42, and we accept it as a serious one: "Be on the alert, for you do not know which day your Lord is coming."

Because Gary and I, and many others who follow Christ, firmly believe the Lord Jesus will return for

His people on a day yet to be known, we sincerely want to be ready for that momentous event. To be fully prepared for His appearing is to make sure the "chambers" of our hearts, so to speak, are filled with the presence of Christ. The apostle Paul wrote, "I bow my knees before the Father [that you will]... know the love of Christ which surpasses knowledge, that you may be filled up to all the fullness of God" (Ephesians 3:14,19). He also wrote, "May the God of peace Himself sanctify you entirely; and may your spirit and soul and body be preserved complete, without blame at the coming of our Lord Jesus Christ" (1 Thessalonians 5:23).

It would not be a laughing matter for any of us to come to the moment when the Lord returns and have our hearts be empty chambers, void of the redeeming Spirit of our Savior. For that reason, right now would be a good time to make sure we're not living our lives "on credit," assuming that we're ready when we haven't acknowledged Jesus' sacrifice for our sins and redemption, asked for His forgiveness and mercy, and invited Him to be our Lord and Savior.

Is it time to slide the bolt open or tilt the cylinder out and do some self-examination? If your life is empty, if it lacks the redemptive and saving grace of Christ, ask Him to load you up. He will!

Lord Jesus, thank You for providing the way to everlasting salvation and peace. My heart up to this point has been empty. Please fill it with the power of Your Spirit so I can enjoy the assurance the apostle John wrote about: "Now...abide in Him, so that when He appears, we may have confidence and not shrink away from Him in shame at His coming. Amen.

74

A Country Boy Testifies

Always [be] ready to…give an account
for the hope that is in you.

1 PETER 3:15

I've been blessed and honored to receive some very nice compliments after speaking and singing at events. Encouragements such as "I enjoyed the music," or "You and your wife sound nice together," or "What kind of guitar do you play…loved the sound of it" warm my heart. But of all the nice things folks have said through the years, my number one favorite is still the feedback I got after a concert in the state of Alabama.

A tall, slim fellow in jeans, boots, and a plaid shirt found me in the hall of the church we were visiting. He held his baseball-style cap in his hand as he began to speak in a thick southern drawl. I'll never forget what he said.

"Mr. Chapman, I didn't wanna come hyar tonite. My wife talked me into it. But I'm sure glad she did." He shifted his weight from one leg to another and added, "And I'll tell you how glad I am I came. I ain't had a chew in two hours!"

I've never succumbed to the habit of chewing tobacco, but I've lived around plenty who are loyally dedicated to the vice. For that reason I know how important a "chaw of 'backer" can be to those who seriously use it. That made me aware of the immensity of this gentleman's unique compliment. Basically he told me that his uninterrupted presence listening to my concert was a major sacrifice he didn't regret making and that two hours "tobaccy" free was a personal accomplishment. I don't know how it gets any better that that.

Though the "ain't had a chew in two hours" compliment tops my list, a "good ol' boy" from North Carolina came really, really close to matching it. He said, "I had a chance to go deer huntin' this evening on a really good farm, but I came to your concert instead. I'm sure glad I did. My wife is too!" Being a rabid and avid fan of the hunt, I know for sure his praise was sincere.

I'm not sure what it is exactly about Southern folk conversation that makes it a little extra fun to hear. Maybe it's a mixture of a humble demeanor with the delivery and the distinctive rise and fall of vocal volume that sets the Southern talker apart.

Another part of the entertainment value in "down home" talk are the word pictures that some guys and gals create.

In many cases, the images that are conjured up for the sake of clear communication are those that come from right where they live and from the things they care most about. One of the best examples I wrote about in the following song. It features an adaptation of a testimony that is straight from the heart of a fellow who resides south of the Mason–Dixon Line.

A Country Boy Testifies

Just like my old muddy pickup truck
Sittin' out in the rain
He washed me and He cleaned me up
And made me new again
And just like my old bluetick hound
Hot out on the trail
He sought me till He caught me
And I'm glad He never fails

He keeps me on His line
Like my old Zebco
And when I try to get away He reels me in
He won't let me go
He keeps me in His sights

Like my old 30-30
And when it comes time to check me in
He'll make me worthy

I remember when my heart was hard like a field
That hadn't been plowed in years
He came 'long and turned that ground
Like I do with my John Deere
And when I ask He shows me where
These boots they ought to be steppin'
And I know He'll lead me down this long dirt road
To the golden streets of heaven

And all the saints say, "Yee haw!"

Lord, thank You for the variety of lives and tongues You've created. Thanks for the many ways You let me say my thanks to You. May I always be faithful to testify to Your great goodness. In Jesus' name, so be it!

75

What's on Your Mind?

*But Jesus, knowing what they were
thinking in their heart...*

LUKE 9:47

The early-morning October chill had a wintry bite that seemed seasonally premature. The warmth that came with the growing sunlight was welcome. But then again, there was a certain dread I sensed with the rising temperature. On one hand (actually on both!), I was glad the warming air was bringing feeling back into my fingers and toes. On a deer-stand, or anywhere else for that matter, that's always a comforting thing. However, I was well aware that the earlier the mercury reached that late-summer level, the sooner the deer would be drawn to their favorite daytime hiding places.

The nine o'clock hour arrived with a more-than-mild heat, and there was no critter movement to speak of. Assuming that the whitetails couldn't resist an early entry into the coziness of their bedding areas, I decided it was time to pack up, head to the truck, and go to my own thicket for a mid-morning siesta. That was the plan...but plans change.

On my walk to my vehicle, I skirted the edge of the boomerang-shaped field I'd been hunting. As I rounded the bend and saw a portion of meadow not visible from my stand, there they were, still up and about! A herd of six deer, all of them of the female gender I'd been hoping to find. I immediately stopped and slowly went to one knee, hoping they hadn't seen me.

None of the group seemed at all nervous as they slowly fed and meandered toward the east side of the field. One by one they disappeared into the edge of the woods. I whispered, "I think you know what's on their minds. Go for it!" With that little bit of self-prodding, I hunkered down and backed out. When I was sure I was out of their field of vision, I stood upright and hightailed it up the logging road to the top of a sizable hill. I was headed to the shadowy center of pine thicket. I knew if I didn't take the time to rest I'd get there before the small herd arrived. I'd have a chance at taking home some fresh venison.

For the sake of brevity, the result of my quickly formed plan is best told by the 45 pounds of ground satisfaction behind the freezer door in my garage.

How did I know that the pine thicket was where

I needed to be? When I saw which side of the field the deer were headed toward as they fed, I had a very good idea what section of woods was on their minds. I'd hunted that property many a day and had inadvertently kicked bedding deer out of that pine thicket more times than I'd like to admit. The best route to it was up the ravine the deer had entered when they left the field. On that day, my guess was right. And I got there in time to sneak inside their bedroom for a successful hunt.

In that October-morning rendezvous is a picture worthy of passing on. When I envision myself as an unsuspecting deer like those I encountered in that meadow and I put Christ as the "hunter," I'm challenged by the reality that as He watches me in the field of this life, He knows my thoughts and is well aware of where they will lead me. However, I'm also comforted by the truth that if my thoughts aren't pure and might lead me into dangerous places, God is ready to offer me guidance to a better way of thinking if I'll just ask. How do I know this? He did it for His disciples!

Some of the disciples were having a rather heated exchange about who was greatest among them. Jesus was able to resolve the matter quickly because of the amazing gift He possessed in knowing the thoughts of their hearts. He was fully aware that in the deepest recesses of their lives those who were engaged in the argument were headed into the dark thicket of pride. To help them avoid the bullet of destruction that awaited their arrival, He brought them back to reality by pulling a child to His side and using the youngster to teach the lesson that is still important for us to understand today: "He who is least among you all will be great" (see Luke 9:46-48 NKJV).

I'm grateful that Jesus knows what I'm thinking. And I'm utterly thankful that He uses His marvelous gift of knowing my thoughts to keep me from going into a thicket where deadly danger awaits. I just need to ask for His help.

O Lord, thank You for keeping an ear to my heart. You know what is on my mind, and yet You love me. Help me hear and follow Your guidance when You want to change my way of thinking and guide me down a different path. In Your name I pray. Amen.

Lyric Credits

Unless otherwise indicated song lyrics were written by Steve Chapman, published by Times & Seasons Music, Inc./BMI. Used by permission.

Steve Chapman, "He's Watching" lyrics, Times & Seasons Music/2007/BMI, admin. by Gaither Copyright Management.

James Alley, "He Never Did Anything" lyrics, published by Times & Seasons Music, Inc./BMI. Used by permission.

"Skipping in the Dark" by Lilah Lehman Gustafson for her sister Winifred Lehman Pierson, written in memory of their father, Tim Lehman. Used by permission.

About the Author

Steve's love of hunting began in his early teens on a weekend when one of his dad's church members invited him to tag along on an October squirrel hunt. Archery is his first choice in the field, followed by a muzzle loader, and then a pistol or rifle. To date, according to Steve's calculations, he's entered the woods before daylight on more than a thousand mornings and hopes to continue that trend for many more years!

Proudly claiming West Virginia as his home state, Steve grew up the son of a preacher. He met his wife, Annie, in junior high school in 1963. In March 1975, they married and settled in Nashville. There they raised their son and daughter, Nathan and Heidi. The day after Heidi married her beau, Emmitt, Nathan proposed to Stephanie. Both couples are happily married and living in Tennessee. Heidi and Emmitt have blessed Steve and Annie with two beautiful granddaughters, Lily and Josie.

Steve is president of S&A Family, Inc., an organization formed to oversee the production of the Chapmans' recorded music. They've had "family life" as the theme of their lyrics since they began singing together in 1980. As Dove Award-winning artists, their schedule sends them to more than 100 cities a year to present concerts and speak.

More Great Books by the Chapman Family

STEVE CHAPMAN

10 Things I Want My Son to Know
365 Things Every Hunter Should Know
Another Look at Life from a Deer Stand
Fish Tales
A Hunter Sets His Sights
A Hunter's Call
A Look at Life from a Deer Stand
A Look at Life from a Deer Stand Gift Edition
Pursuing the Prize
Quiet Moments for Your Soul
With God on a Deer Hunt

STEVE AND ANNIE CHAPMAN

What Husbands and Wives Aren't Telling Each Other

ANNIE CHAPMAN

10 Things I Want My Daughter to Know
10 Things I Want My Husband to Know
The Mother-in-Law Dance
A Woman's Answer to Anger

ANNIE CHAPMAN AND HEIDI CHAPMAN BEAL

Entertaining Angels

To read sample chapters, go to
www.harvesthousepublishers.com

These books are available at your local
Christian bookstore or you can order them at
www.SteveandAnnieChapman.com

Discography of the Chapman Family

At the Potter's House

An Evening Together

Dogwood…Down the Road

Every Moment

Family Favorites

Finish Well

For Times Like These

Gotta Get There

Hymns from God's Great Cathedral

Kiss of Hearts

Long Enough to Know

Love Was Spoken

The Miles

A Mother's Touch

Nathan Paul

Never Turn Back

Silver Bridge

Steppin' in the Tracks

That Way Again

This House Still Stands

Tools for the Trade

Waiting to Hear

To hear the Chapmans' music, see available products
(CDs/cassettes/videos/books),
find out where they're performing, or
get more information, check out:

www.SteveandAnnieChapman.com

or write to

S&A Family, Inc.
PO Box 535
Madison, TN 37116